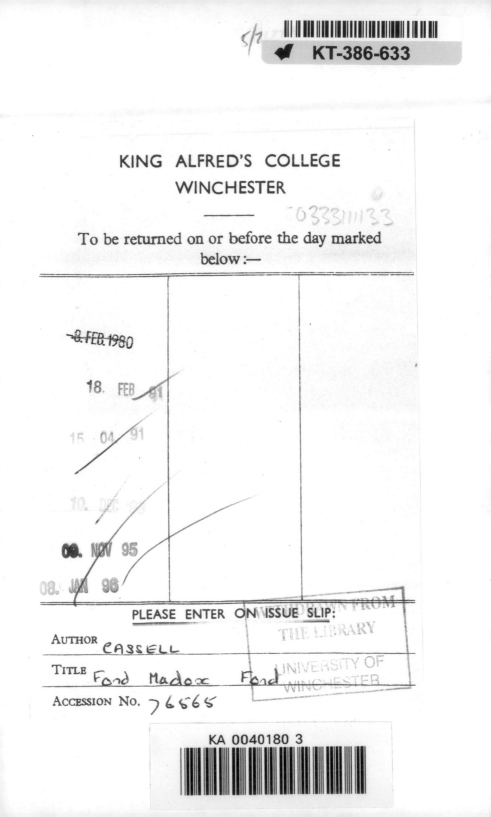

Modern Judgements

FORD MADOX FORD

MODERN JUDGEMENTS

General Editor: P. N. FURBANK

Dickens   A. E. Dyson
Ford Madox Ford   Richard A. Cassell
Henry James   Tony Tanner
Marvell   M. Wilding
Milton   Alan Rudrum
Sean O'Casey   Ronald Ayling
Pasternak   Donald Davie and Angela Livingstone
Racine   R. C. Knight
Walter Scott   D. D. Devlin
Shelley   R. B. Woodings
Swift   A. Norman Jeffares

IN PREPARATION
Freud   F. Cioffi

Ford Madox Ford

MODERN JUDGEMENTS

edited by

RICHARD A. CASSELL

MACMILLAN

First published 1972 by
THE MACMILLAN PRESS LTD
London and Basingstoke
Associated companies in New York Toronto
Dublin Melbourne Johannesburg and Madras

SBN 333 11113 3

Printed in Great Britain by
HAZELL WATSON AND VINEY LTD
Aylesbury, Bucks

To the memory of Morton Dauwen Zabel

Contents

Acknowledgements

'Ford Madox Ford: Obit' by Ezra Pound from *Homage to Ford Madox Ford*, New Directions, no. 7, copyright 1942 by New Directions Publishing Corporation, reprinted by permission of New Directions Publishing Corporation, New York, agents for Dorothy Pound, Committee for Ezra Pound; extract from an article by Edward Crankshaw from *National Review*, CXXXI (1948), by permission of A. D. Peters & Co.; 'The Last Pre-Raphaelite' by Morton Dauwen Zabel from *Craft and Character in Modern Fiction* by Morton Dauwen Zabel, copyright 1949, 1957 by Morton Dauwen Zabel, by permission of the Viking Press, Inc.; 'Tietjens in Disguise' by R. W. Lid from *The Kenyon Review*, XXII, copyright 1960, reprinted by permission of the Regents of the University of California; '*The Good Soldier*; an interpretation' by Mark Schorer reprinted by permission of Farrar, Straus & Giroux, Inc., and A. M. Heath & Co. Ltd, from *The World We Imagine* by Mark Schorer, copyright 1948, 1968 by Mark Schorer; 'The Saddest Story' by John A. Meixner from *Ford Madox Ford's Novels* (Minneapolis: University of Minnesota Press), copyright 1962 by the University of Minnesota; Mr Samuel Hynes for 'The Epistemology of *The Good Soldier*' by Samuel Hynes from *Sewanee Review*, LXIX (spring 1961); 'Image, Identity, and Insight in *The Good Soldier*' by Jo-Ann Baernstein from *Critique*, IX (1966) Studies in Modern Fiction; '*Parade's End*' by William Carlos Williams from *Selected Essays*, copyright 1954 by William Carlos Williams, reprinted by permission of New Directions Publishing Corporation, New York; 'A Double Reading of *Parade's End*' by Marlene Griffith from *Modern Fiction Studies*, IX, copyright 1963 by Purdue Research Foundation, Lafayette, Indiana; 'Persecution and Paranoia in *Parade's End*' by Melvin Seiden reprinted from *Criticism*, VIII (summer 1966) by permission of Wayne State University Press; 'The Poetics of Speech' by Hugh Kenner © Hugh Kenner 1972; 'To Ford Madox Ford in Heaven' by William Carlos Williams from *Collected Later Poems*, copyright 1944 by William Carlos Williams, reprinted by permission of New Directions Publishing Corporation, New York, and MacGibbon & Kee Ltd.

General Editor's Preface

LITERARY criticism has only recently come of age as an academic discipline, and the intellectual activity that, a hundred years ago, went into theological discussion, now finds its most natural outlet in the critical essay. Amid a good deal that is dull or silly or pretentious, every year now produces a crop of critical essays which are brilliant and profound not only as contributions to the understanding of a particular author but as statements of an original way of looking at literature and the world. Hence, it often seems that the most useful undertaking for an academic publisher might be, not so much to commission new books of literary criticism or scholarship, as to make the best of what exists easily available. This at least is the purpose of the present series of anthologies, each of which is devoted to a single major writer.

The guiding principle of selection is to assemble the best *modern* criticism—broadly speaking, that of the last twenty or thirty years—and to include historic and classic essays, however famous, only when they are still influential and represent the best statements of their particular point of view. It will, however, be one of the functions of the editor's Introduction to sketch in the earlier history of criticism in regard to the author concerned.

Each volume will attempt to strike a balance between general essays and ones on specialised aspects, or particular works, of the writer in question. And though in many instances the bulk of the articles will come from British and American sources, certain of the volumes will draw heavily on material in other European languages—most of it being translated for the first time.

P. N. FURBANK

Introduction

THE name of Ford Madox Ford in the past two decades has made a slow progress into the ranks of modern literary figures. He has emerged not so much from total obscurity as from a hushed silence, a reticence brought on by critical shortsightedness, literary politics, the jealousies and egos of his friends and foes, and Ford himself. Ford lived in the shade of others: of his Pre-Raphaelite and Victorian forebears, of Conrad, James, Pound, Joyce, Hemingway. When he most came into the light, he was the agent of scandal or controversy, notably during his tragi-comic affair with Violet Hunt, which was not soon forgotten, and after his book on Conrad, which was not soon forgiven, at least by Conrad apologists.

Though well known in London's artistic community before World War I and in Paris in the twenties, few of his books made enough to cover his advances; he constantly had to seek out publishers, and even his few boomings in the Press usually resulted in more noise than sales. After the war, and in the backwash of the Violet Hunt scandal, ignored or condemned by many in his circle, and indignant at the government he saw as betraying the principles over which the war had been fought, he exiled himself to France and the United States, returning to England only for short visits. He died relatively obscure, nearly penniless, and with no collected works on the shelf—in fact, with most of his books out of print. Yet we are beginning to see that neither Ford nor his life was as disastrous as many have said. He led a hard-working life dedicated to literature and enjoyed a measure of good luck and success, if not financial solvency, during the *English Review* days (1908–10) and after publication of the Tietjens' novels in the twenties. He lived through the trials he caused and suffered with a remarkable resilience, and though he wrote much that fell below his own standards, it is questionable whether he seriously compromised his art, at least for long. As a writer he wrote, always aware of his talents with the pen, and usually capable of judging their value. His record is enviable. Despite lapses and actual bad writing, the bulk of his work from the beginning (1891) to the end (1938) is well written and even when trivial is entertaining. He never wrote a totally worthless book or essay or poem.

Today there are hopeful signs that Ford has an increasing audience of readers among students and younger scholars. Once aware of his work, they are interested and are especially attracted to *The Good Soldier*. They find he distrusted the establishment in politics, economics and letters; hated the mechanical, the selfish, the oppressive; deplored the modern breakdown in clear communication, and foresaw the frustrating gaps and polarities that plague and separate us today. The young can appreciate Ford's seeking serenity out of anxiety and can respect him for his horror of war, for his intense awareness of sham and deceit in society, for his willingness to change and seek new beginnings, and for his penetrating dramatisation of sexual life without Victorian evasion or the current verbal display. The older generation can accuse Ford of being a champion for lost causes known to be lost, as R. P. Blackmur once did, but the young find in him lost causes to be rediscovered and then reshaped. In fact, they are finding him contemporary. Several younger critics, for example, are reading *The Good Soldier* as an early existential document of personal anguish and despair that defines the human condition amid twentieth-century absurdity. Invariably they quote Dowell's lament: 'We are all so afraid, we are all so alone, we all so need from the outside the assurance of our own worthiness to exist'; and find relevant Ford's prison world 'full of screaming hysterics, tied down so that we might not outsound the rolling of our carriage wheels'. In addition, books like *Parade's End*, *No Enemy*, *Provence*, *Great Trade Route* speak to the young in their quest for understanding and compassion.

As for Ford's contemporaries, it is evident that his personality, or the reports of it, often stood in the way of reading his work. He was an enigma of paradoxes. His friend Ezra Pound once said that Ford had all the virtues but seldom could call the right ones into service at the right time. An overbearing self-assurance periodically obscured his constant need for love and support—from women, colleagues and the public. He was generous with his money, his sympathies, his talents, and careless in business and personal affairs. He inspired affection, but often exhausted the emotions of those who admired or loved him. He transformed literal fact in order to capture impressionistic reality, and he told lies because they made good stories. Endowed with a hyperactive imagination and easily touched sensibilities, he asserted or protected himself by a variety of public poses, from lord of the manor to small farmer, from Bohemian to dandy, from *le jeune homme modeste* (as he says James called him) to *le cher Maître* (as he called James). Both an incisive analyst of emotions and a sentimentalist, his works are character-ised by his sardonic yet comic vision of the depletions and agonies of his time, and by his simple ideals and compassionate hopes, on occasion made precarious by doubts approaching despair for man and his future. A complicated collection of perceptions and insensitivities, of intellect and emotions, of talents and ineptitudes, Ford fascinated and perplexed both those who knew him and those who read him.

'A great system of assumed *personas* and dramatized selves,' H. G. Wells described him in 1934, implying that in his masks and poses Ford, 'after the stresses of war,' bordered on madness. Earlier, in his literary spoof *Boon* (1915), Wells presents Ford as 'the Only Uncle of the Gifted Young . . . now boasting about trivialities, and now making familiar criticisms (which are invariably ill-received), and occasionally quite absent-mindedly producing splendid poetry'. Almost without ex-ception, contemporaries trying to capture Ford's personality and presence were forced into metaphor. Well known is Norman Douglas's reference to Ford 'as so fat and Buddhistic and nasal that a dear friend described him as an animated adenoid. Adenoid or no, he remained good company.' Equally well known is D. H. Lawrence's writing in a letter that Ford 'daubs his dove-grey kindliness with a villainous selfish tar, and hops forth a very rook among rooks, but his eyes, after all, 'remain like the Shulamite's, dove's eyes'.[1] He has been likened to Gargantua, Timon and Falstaff, Dr Jekyll and Mr Hyde, Humpty-Dumpty, Lord Plushbottom. But usually those who knew him were impressed by his resemblance to some massive sea or land animal: 'a friendly walrus', 'a leviathan', 'a behemoth in grey tweeds', 'an un-forgetting elephant', 'a flabby lemon and pink giant, who hung his mouth open as though he were an animal at the Zoo inviting buns'. With some wit and ingenuousness, Ford adopted many of his friends' epi-thets for himself and for those of his characters who resembled him: like Tietjens, 'the motionless carp', 'the whale', 'the dear meal-sack elephant'.

[1] To Violet Hunt. Quoted in *The Flurried Years* (1926) p. 158.

These remarks, born of affection and irritation, probably had little effect on his public reputation. But books published in his lifetime by two different, equally vindictive women did cause Ford profound anguish and great harm. In successive volumes on her husband, Mrs Jessie Conrad became increasingly critical of Ford. What most aroused her indignation was Ford's impressionistic reminiscence of Conrad, a book he wrote immediately after Conrad's death, with what must have been mixed emotions, yet with a justice and a humility that looked to her like presumption. Grudgingly admitting Ford to be a man of talent once useful as a 'mental stimulus', Mrs Conrad could not admit that Conrad owed much of a debt to Ford. She dismissed Ford as a liar and the memoir as 'that detested book'. The counterbalance was long in coming. Some critics, like G. Jean-Aubry and R. L. Mégroz, followed Mrs Conrad's path; others, like Edward Garnett, Wells and Mencken, who was not favourably disposed to Ford, generally defended the memoir and Ford's role in the collaboration. But it was not until 1959 that Jocelyn Baines, in his biography of Conrad, in seeking out all the facts of the collaboration, concluded that Conrad's meeting with Ford in 1898 was 'the most important event in Conrad's literary career'. A year later Frederick Karl was to declare that after 'Conrad forsook the theories he worked out with Ford and those he expressed in his early letters and essays ... his work became thin and uninteresting'. Karl agrees with Pound that the two men devised the 'New Novel' and influenced the course of English fiction.

The other woman, Violet Hunt, publicly expressed her love-hate, admiration-despair in a distraught, inaccurate, paranoid but fascinating defence of her years with Ford, titled with the grace of understatement *The Flurried Years* (1926; with less grace published in America as *I Have This to Say*.) She complained of Ford's betrayal of her and their love, and she resentfully conceded herself as a model for Sylvia Tietjens, a connection which her book confirms. Ford was now a bounder as well as a liar. He himself kept a gentlemanly silence, but, as Meixner suggests, her public cry, along with Mrs Conrad's attack launched about the same time, might have helped precipitate the decline in Ford's creative talents after the first volume of the Tietjens' series, *Some Do Not*.[1]

[1] Ford was luckier with the more tender, penetrating record, *Drawn from Life* (1941), by Stella Bowen, with whom he lived for several years after the war. But her book did not appear until two years after Ford's death.

Ford's reputation was hurt as much by the silence of important
colleagues as it was by the outspokenness of these forthright ladies.
Henry James said nothing about the man or his work, and Conrad very
little, at least in public statements, and they damned him by their
silence. Even the well-known protégés, with the exceptions of Pound
and Douglas Goldring, restricted most of their comments to letters and
offered only their judgements of him as editor and friend, not evalua-
tions of his writing. Lawrence never published a word on Ford's work,
and Norman Douglas published only two appreciative but anonymous
reviews.

The major share of critical response to Ford's work during his lifetime offered cautious admiration tempered by reservation, sometimes
damning.[1] From the earliest journalistic reviewers, critics have generally
respected Ford's skill with words and cadences in achieving fresh and
notable effects. Often to admire, sometimes to condemn, critics have
commented on his 'preciosity', his 'finely hammered', 'artificial' style.
'Tours de force', 'brilliant', 'clever' are early and late epithets in Fordian
criticism, sometimes with the related observations that there is more
style than content, more art than life, more excellence in parts than
perfection in the whole.

Despite Ford's absence from the ranks of even the minor British poets,
where he seems rightfully to belong, his poetry was accepted by his
contemporary critics as innovative and modern. H. G. Wells claimed
Ford was an unrecognised great poet; 'On Heaven', 'Antwerp', among
a few other poems, were singled out for praise. Critics like Milton
Bronner saw that Ford's 'noun-and-verb verse' anticipated the Imagists,
a judgement later confirmed by Stanley Coffman, Noel Stock, Hugh
Kenner and Pound himself. Most critics have commented on the
similarity between Ford's poetic and prose styles, reflecting his theory
of a literary language as somewhat heightened and refined conversation;
some, like Conrad Aiken, complained; others, like John Peale Bishop
and Ezra Pound, approved.

Pound, Ford's oldest and most faithful champion, shouted persistently
into deaf ears that before Joyce 'the revolution of the word began . . .

[1] The best survey of Ford's journalistic and critical reputation can be found in David
Dow Harvey's thorough, indispensable bibliography, which quotes from and summarises
almost every published comment on Ford from 1891 to 1962. In my introduction,
references not documented are either easily traceable in Harvey, or listed in the bibliography at the end of this volume.

with the LONE whimper of Ford Madox Hueffer'. Pound praised Ford
for insisting 'upon clarity and precision, upon the prose tradition', and
for teaching that 'one should write in a contemporary spoken or at least
a speakable language'. Though Pound was always suspicious of impressionism ('impressionism belongs in paint, it is of the eye'), he later
admitted that out of Ford's impressionism, 'whereinto come only
colours, concrete forms, tones of voice, modes of gesture . . .' one builds
a 'sane ideogram'.

Pound defended Ford as a literary man, and more for his ideas, his
skill, his integrity than for his creative work as either poet or novelist.
He admired several poems and the novel *A Call*; otherwise Ford's 'own
best prose was probably lost as isolated chapters in unachieved and too-
quickly-issued novels'. But Pound could go as far as to call Ford 'the
best critic in England, one might say the only critic of any importance',
at a time when Gosse and Saintsbury headed the critical establishment
and Hulme led the new classicism, favoured by Eliot and Pound himself. As late as 1938, Pound was still claiming that 'the critical LIGHT
during the years immediately pre-war in London shone not from Hulme
but from Ford . . . in so far as it fell on writing at all', a judgement still
challenged, though recently confirmed in some measure by Frank
MacShane and Miss Cyrena Pondrom. Pound, however, objected to
the impressionistic visual focus of Ford's criticism and to Ford's theory
of 'narrative objectivity and disappearance' and suggested that Ford's
failure as a critic derived from his 'wholly unpolitic generosity'.

Other critics have challenged Ford's critical tactics. Rebecca West
questioned that he was a great critic 'because of his transforming
memory which altered everything' and could not recall a single book
as it was written.[1] Dixon Scott, reviewing Ford's book on James (1914),
argued that Ford was trying to enlist James in Ford's lesser camp and
within his own 'dark grudge against humanity', a need which led Ford
to 'the unconscious queering of evidence, the fakings and suppressions'.
Both Rebecca West and Scott were in effect complaining of Ford's
writing criticism and literary reminiscence as fiction, a practice which
naturally allows the 'transforming memory' full play. Most critics have
long resisted this unorthodox approach, but we may come to see that
Ford's experiments in impressionistic criticism and biography helped

---

[1] Quoted in Frank MacShane's Introduction to *Critical Writings of Ford Madox Ford*
(Lincoln, Nebraska, 1964) p. xiii.

set some precedents, perhaps for the currently popular non-fiction novel (or fictional non-fiction), and certainly for fictional confessions like Hemingway's *A Moveable Feast,* which one reviewer has already labelled as Hemingway's best novel. Ford's criticism is more than 'a by-product of his imaginative work', as MacShane says;[1] it is rather one form of it, and if idiosyncratic and inaccurate, it is also knowing and perceptive.

In the thirties, Graham Greene and V. S. Pritchett took up Ford's cause and established challenges for subsequent academic criticism of his work. Pritchett, the more reserved in his admiration, felt that Ford's work shows an obsession with technique and that it more often dazzles than illuminates. Not until Ford was freed from the Pre-Raphaelite confusion of painting with writing and from the influences of James and Conrad, could he achieve what Pritchett describes as the 'determined stupor out of which greater novelists work', and then only in *The Fifth Queen, The Good Soldier* and parts of *Parade's End.* Further, Pritchett charged that Ford's brilliance masks an absence of compassion. Ford 'is a festive and gregarious mind but not a heart', whose novels leave us pained, Pritchett concluded, but without the purgation of passion.

Graham Greene wrote of Ford with profound respect for him as an artist combined with an affection usually reserved for a kindly, wayward uncle. 'A fine writer,' Greene called him, 'with traces of a most engaging charlatan.' Once he even praised Ford as 'our finest living novelist', who was 'not only a designer; he was a carpenter: you feel in his work the love of the tools and the love of the material'. With an eye for danger, Greene claimed that Ford taught Conrad techniques the old master used 'more stiffly and less skilfully' than the young teacher. In addition, Ford extended his experiments in point of view beyond those of James, and in his fictional method 'has something in common with Mr Pound's *Cantos*—simultaneity, but carried out with infinitely greater technical ability'. Greene was one of the first critics to accept Ford's impressionism in both his fiction and memoirs for what it is: Ford's own personal impression of life founded on his artist's insistence that stories be well told, with facts subservient to the effect (a manner Greene calls 'atmospheric'). Perceiving the paradoxical quality of Ford's temperament, Greene has argued that Ford's impressionism was drawn from his 'hilarious imagination', which gives to his works their

[1] Introduction to *Critical Writings,* p. xiii.

'unmistakable . . . stamp—the outrageous fancy, the pessimistic high spirits', or the 'hilarious depression', as he also phrases it. Perhaps Greene's most seminal insight is that *The Good Soldier* and *Parade's End* are 'almost the only adult novels dealing with the sexual life that have been written in English. They are almost our only reply to Flaubert.'[1] Subsequently, critics like R. W. Lid, Jo-Ann Baernstein and Thomas Moser, by exploring Ford's sexual themes, have begun to discover more precisely the nature of that reply.

Pound and Greene, virtually alone among literary figures, marked the event of Ford's death in 1939 with fond, perceptive tributes. His memory was kept alive in the forties by Stella Bowen's and Douglas Goldring's biographical accounts, a memorial homage by literary friends published by New Directions (1942), a Ford issue of the Princeton *Library Chronicle* (1948), and by Penguin British editions of *The Good Soldier* and the Tietjens' novels. Encouraged by this activity and the critical response to Goldring's books, Knopf issued both the Tietjens tetralogy, under the title *Parade's End* (1950), and *The Good Soldier* (1951). Despite a flurry of publicity, a hoped-for revival did not materialise. But these reprintings sparked an extensive critical examination beginning in the late fifties, mostly by young American critics, who in numerous books, articles and dissertations paid most attention to the novels and revealed a master whose technical dexterity and thematic complexity proved both demanding and rewarding.

As these critics have investigated the various elements in Ford's fiction, we have been brought to see that though Ford is a personal writer, he is not merely that, and that though wise and knowledgeable in his art, he is more than that. At his best, the created worlds of his stories and impressions have the power to sharpen our senses and our mind, to transform our awareness, and to modify, perhaps renew, or even reshape our understanding of the worlds we live in—or create for ourselves—individually and collectively. The overall critical assessment is favourable. Ford has now finally been accorded his rightfully secure if not foremost position among modern novelists.

Almost all critics agree that *The Good Soldier* and *Parade's End* are not only Ford's masterpieces but are also masterworks of the twentieth century. Rediscovered as he was in the aftersurge of the James revival

---

[1] In a publicity brochure of Knopf, 1950.

and the impressive Lubbock defence of the Jamesian method, attention was initially given to Ford's fictional technique. *Le mot juste*, the time shift, *progression d'effet*, justification, juxtaposition, point of view, surprise, the key terms of Ford's literary method, were thoroughly explored, as several essays in this volume illustrate. Criticism has naturally emphasised Ford's development from apprentice to craftsman as he slowly freed himself of Pre-Raphaelite, Jamesian, Conradian and Continental influences. He never quite did this, of course, for influences are not so easily traceable as we like them to be, and Ford's talent, as some of the early novels show, could be remarkably independent. But Lid and others have recognised that for all the talk and work with Conrad that brought Ford's technical theories into full life, the most noticeable influence among living writers on Ford was James. Other influences seem strongly at work, especially those of Flaubert and Maupassant. Critics have discovered traces of writers from Richardson to Hemingway, and also from Dante, Shakespeare and the Restoration dramatists, but saying as much says relatively little, except to place Ford in the tradition he admired as well as in the *avant garde* of his day.[1] If *Parade's End* seems to fit more snugly into the English mould, *The Good Soldier* is among the most original of English novels.

Glimmerings of originality—on occasion blazes, as in the 'Fifth Queen' trilogy—light up the early novels (1891–1914). Ford later labelled them *pastiches*, *tours de force*, potboilers, which in many ways they are when compared to his major fiction. But the early novels offer more than experiments in technical virtuosity; they show us Ford in search of a subject that will fully capture his creative imagination. Brought up rather aimlessly in a somewhat rarefied Pre-Raphaelite, Victorian artistic atmosphere that stifled him, Ford needed a kind of collision with reality—his own reality—to draw on in order to create a vital imaginative world. That collision apparently came first during his trials of love and then of war, trials which happened much later in his life than they did, say, for Hemingway, who perhaps more fortunately found his subject as he was learning to write.

[1] See, for example, James T. Cox, 'The Finest French Novel in the English Language', in *Modern Fiction Studies*, IX (1963); R. W. Lid, 'Ford Madox Ford, Flaubert and the English Novel', in *Spectrum*, VI (1962); and H. R. Huntley, 'Ford, Holbein, and Dürer', in *South Atlantic Bulletin*, XXX (1965), and '*The Good Soldier* and *Die Wahlve wandtschaften*' in *Comparative Literature*, XIX (1967), which argues Ford's extensive bor owing from Goethe's novel.

Ford's imagination was charged by his agonised involvements in love and later the war, though the war in his work is less a matter of trenches and bullets than of the trials of love shifted to a different battleground. Supported by his considerable powers as a craftsman, he transcended the early fairy tales and historical and contemporary romances to achieve the masterpieces of his middle years. As Caroline Gordon and Ambrose Gordon, Jr. have argued, the major novels retain strong elements of the fairy tale and romance, may be in fact contemporary analogues of myth and fairy tale, but their writing finally allowed Ford to arrive at the subject, I think his true subject, that had long intrigued him. His subject is not strictly love and war at all, but rather the trial of private lives inextricably caught up in the tangles of civilisation. His protagonists, usually gentry or 'good people', experience the frustration of trying to live their own lives while having to live with others trying to do the same, and in a civilised, convention-bound society that had shaped and apparently captured them all but is rotting at the centre.

Men of sentiment or passion, or both, trained to a hand-me-down devotion for feudal and courtly ideals, face betrayal and dismissal by a society that has relinquished those ideals and made of modern life a frightful struggle for self-survival. Once they give in to their sentiments and passions, usually to a contemporary descendant of a Lamia-like temptress, a *Belle Dame sans merci*, his heroes are brought to renunciation and then to defeat or reconstruction, to use Ford's word. The careers of Ford's protagonists and antagonists are intensively examined in Caroline Gordon's 'A Good Soldier', James Cox's 'Ford's Passion for Provence', and the books by Norman Leer and H. Robert Huntley. A deep thematic current, not directly on the surface for long except in the 'Fifth Queen' novels, is the political struggle between Catholic and Protestant, Catholic and Catholic, the wayward and the devout. Though Ford is always more concerned with how these struggles affect private emotional and sexual lives, his characters are clearly heirs—even victims—of religious history since the Albigensian heresy and the Reformation and cannot fully be understood without reference to those religious upheavals. Several critics have begun to explore the moral and psychological trials of this religious heritage on Ford's characters: most notably Meixner, James Hafley, Daniel R. Barnes and Andreach. A more overt theme that amounts to a shattering indictment of modern life is that of the lack of clear communication, a breakdown of haunting

worry to an artist like Ford, who long brooded over failures in intellectual and emotional communication. William Carlos Williams,
among a very few, has recognised the centrality of this concern in Ford's
work.

Ford was characteristically a romantic temperament who sought and
found a realistic literary method. He was a man of dreams, visions and
ideals who felt compelled to leave a record of his age, an age in which
those dreams, visions and ideals were tarnished when not lost. Once his
imaginative world was ready, Ford wrote his best novels and created a
revelatory symbolic picture—or cinema—of modern life. If it is true
that he developed a fictional theory and technique before finding his
real subject, it is unfair to assume that he had merely collected a bag of
tricks, or even that his best work can be analysed solely in terms of his
writings on technique. In *The Good Soldier* and *Parade's End*, perhaps
above all others, technique in fact seems a process of discovery.

The Good Soldier in particular has been a fascinating treasure chest for
critics. Even though the novel's intricacies of technique and design
repelled or baffled most of its earliest reviewers, Rebecca West wrote of
'its extreme beauty and wisdom . . . a noble and ambitious design . . .
never once does it appear as the work of man's invention'. For her the
book is 'the record of the spiritual life of Edward Ashburnham' told by
'a terrible and wholly credible American, a cold and controlled egoist'.
Theodore Dreiser, the only American to give his name to a review of
the first edition (in the *New Republic*), felt rather it is the narrative that
is 'cold' and 'never truly poignant', that 'Dowell is no American', is in
fact a projection of Ford, and that the influence of Conrad and the
'encrusting formalism which, barnaclewise is apparently overtaking
and destroying all that is best in English life' ruin it. On the other hand,
he did see the novel as 'tragic in the best sense that the Greeks knew
tragedy, that tragedy for which there is no solution'.

An American reprint of 1927 elicited only one review and that from
Clifton Fadiman, who saw the novel as a kind of fossil and the characters
as 'a complete set of museum pieces'. Nevertheless, in a concession he
must have offered as faint praise, he admitted that the novel 'is prefer-
able to James at his best'. By the end of the decade, only Hugh Walpole
and Granville Hicks were raising their voices in support of the novel.
Hicks argued that *The Good Soldier* 'is not merely a *tour de force*', and
that in complexity of subject it went beyond Conrad, and in its 'intense

and volcanic' exploration of emotion beyond James. But *The Good Soldier* rested underground until several years after Ford's death.

The initial reception of the 1951 Knopf reprint was as unimpressive as that of the first edition: Harvey lists only seven reviews, one by an Englishman and all in American publications. Amazed by its technical virtuosity, the reviewers who deigned to give it notice repeated the tired epithets of 'marvellous', 'brilliant', 'a *tour de force*', and so on. Two of the better critics reviewing the novel, Pritchett and Hugh Kenner, resorted to the mechanical image of the turning of the screw to explain the impact of the novel's method, and both suggested the screw is turned too tightly. Using Mark Schorer's introductory essay (first published in somewhat different form in 1948) as a base of operation, but actually more often like an enemy target, later critics have explored Ford's narrative techniques and argued back and forth on the reliability of Dowell as narrator and on just what we can make of him and the novel.

The critics have raised more questions than answers. Is the novel an ironic comedy of humours (Schorer), a high comedy with tragic undertones (as I once suggested), a tragedy around whose tragic core Ford 'placed a context of comic irony' (Meixner), or 'a savage comedy of manners' (Bort)? The question of whether or not the narrator Dowell is reliable has inspired the most fervent inquiry: he is and he isn't, most say, yet both have been argued separately. Inevitably, the quest to define the narrator has expanded into an examination of the epistemological process, of the fallibility of human knowledge of self and of others (Hafley and Hynes), of Dowell as an earnest seeker, groping without full insight in a mythic darkness (Hanzo) rather than a passive, confused recorder suffering from fatigue and moral inertia (Schorer), or a 'psychic cripple' unable to act yet complex with feeling (Meixner). What is the moral norm or centre of the novel: Dowell's fallibility (Hynes), Dowell as a 'literal-minded, alienated, rootless creature of the modern Christless age' (Andreach), Ashburnham and Nancy (Hafley), the Provençal ethic (Cox), or the courtly love tradition of the Protestant-Provençal-Albigensian Ashburnham victimised by the debased Catholic Leonora (Barnes)? According to the interpretation, Leonora is the villain, or Florence, or Ashburnham, or Dowell when he is the bad Protestant, a kind of ally to Leonora, the bad Catholic, or when he is not the dupe or the seeker for truth, or both. Who, in fact, is the protagonist? Most say Ashburnham; some, like Arthur Mizener, suggest both Dowell and Ashburnham (Ford's two selves separated); some other recent critics, like Todd Bender and Sondra Stang, argue for Dowell, that the novel is about the way his mind works, that in his search for understanding he achieves 'potency and effectiveness' and becomes a kind of rhetorical instrument for depicting Ford's existential view of the human predicament.

Among those critics who accept *The Good Soldier* as a masterpiece, some, like Meixner and Lid, accept it because it is nearly a perfect fusion of technique and subject; some, like Cox, because it isn't, since Ford had set out to expose Ashburnham, the symbol of courtly love obsolete in the modern world, and ended by praising him. Several other critics, seeking for biographical connections as keys to the novel, have explored the moral, intellectual and psychological patterns that help define Ford's temperament and the nature of his art. They offer no clear answer except that Dowell, Ford and his protagonists are in some way connected. A critic like Mrs Carol Ohmann argues that after a troublesome apprenticeship, Ford by the time of *The Good Soldier* had drawn his true subject and convictions out of his unconscious mind and was able to treat his characters' emotional and moral bewilderment both compassionately and objectively. On the other hand, a critic like Kenner perceives less distance between Ford and Dowell, since Ford suffers from 'an impasse of sympathy for all sides' that reveals Dowell's suspension of judgement to be in fact Ford's own bewilderment.

Of course, not all these interpretations will prove incompatible with each other in a total view that might be achieved of *The Good Soldier*, once its 'irresolvable pluralism of truths', as Hynes phrases it, is explored and the novel is seen on all its possible levels of meaning. But the enigmas the novel still poses to its critics warn us we have much to learn and understand. We do not yet know enough about Ford or how he worked or what he drew upon from his experience, both real and imagined. The biographies published so far, though extremely helpful, do not tell us all we need to know when faced with *The Good Soldier* and Ford's finest work. Douglas Goldring's two books (*South Lodge* and the much less adequate *Trained for Genius*) offer a perceptive, intimate portrait by one who once knew Ford well, but they are avowedly uncritical. Frank MacShane's 1965 biography, a valuable source for its revelations of the outer public man, drawn mostly from those who knew him, is lacking in its analysis of the inner man, the artist, and, further, MacShane dismisses *The Good Soldier* as 'too much like a novel by Henry James reworked by Ford'. Arthur Mizener's *The Saddest Story* (1971) is the most critically responsible, the most thorough, the most informative of the biographies. Yet his analysis of *The Good Soldier*, though reserved and level-headed, is incomplete; but because he increases our knowledge of the novel's connections with Ford's life and temperament, it does set a necessary cornerstone for subsequent critical examination.

Already we know enough to realise that *The Good Soldier* offers more than a mere chilling technical display of brilliant fireworks that falls short of greatness. To be sure, there is a chilling justice that controls *The Good Soldier*—what Ford called inevitability—where no basis for regeneration exists, as it will in *Parade's End*. Possibly such a dead end results from Kenner's 'impasse of sympathy', or if Ford is in some way both Dowell and Ashburnham, who offer, in Walter Allen's phrase, 'objective correlatives of Ford's own emotional situations', then maybe both sides of Ford at this time had to cancel each other out or be paralysed, a paralysis he will transfer to Mark Tietjens alone in *Last Post*. More likely, his insight, perhaps inspired by his personal involvements, revealed to him the paralysis fragmenting and exhausting modern society. Whatever the reason, paralysis and justice and sympathy are in *The Good Soldier*, but it is not a cold narrative. It is in fact an impassioned tale of passion—of passions—under remarkable artistic control.

Dowell is no Jake Barnes, yet he is a man emasculated before the war, in part by virtue of his being an American, a nationality Ford once characterised as sexless. Hynes sees Dowell as ironically the only one in the novel capable of love; if so, the capacity is potential, realised mostly in sentimental responses, as is evidenced by both his rather dark cynicism and his emulation of Ashburnham. The narrator as cuckold-nursemaid discovering the grim facts of his own life, eager to know, dispossessed of his illusions, though still clinging to a few, telling a tale of a shattering expense of passion and telling it with anguished honesty and astonishment creates perhaps one of the warmest, even most poignant, documents of its time, if these clichés can still connote that fusion of compassion and pain, both of the mind and the senses, that pervades the novel and takes over the reader. Wiley, in discussing the mental suffering inherent in Ford's 'affairs', cites Ford's remark that

'impressions are sensations that impinge and leave scars on the consciousness . . .' That says it more precisely. The passion is in the book and in
the ironic way of telling so that the reader doesn't need to know a fact
of Ford's life to experience it. For those who know something of Ford
comes the understanding that his technical facility had not only found
the submerged subject he had long been searching for, but also that by
means of his facility—or genius—Ford finally discovered the voice for
his own anguish and the clarity of vision such discipline can impose.

The grimness of the novel is not itself self-pity or a sentimental
evasion, though it could have been either. It is rather an illumination
and of the kind explained by Stella Bowen's remark in a more personal
connection: 'He could show you two sides simultaneously of any
human affair, and the double picture made the subject come alive, and
stand out in a third-dimensional way that was very exciting.' I suspect
that it is, in fact, as Miss Gordon tells us, the Euripidean irresolution,
where no purgation is allowed. Or it is the Flaubertian resolution of
Madame Bovary, where the agony is prolonged. Certainly, no reassurance
is possible after reading Ford's record of the psychological devastation
that resulted from emotions imprisoned by a rigidly structured and
codified society, or after experiencing the exhausting sadness of the
death of the traditional honour and punctilio which sustained that
structure and that code.

Parade's End seems an easier work—in a way, a more conventional
one. Critics have been better able to attach it to some familiar novel:
Vanity Fair, the *Forsyte Saga*, Balzac's *La Comédie Humaine*, *L'Éduca-
tion Sentimentale* have all been mentioned; others have connected it with
Dorothy Richardson's *Pilgrimage* or *À la Recherche du Temps Perdu*, or,
more obviously, Mottram's *The Spanish Farm*. By itself, *Parade's End*
holds fewer enigmas than *The Good Soldier*, has clearer lines more
easily seen, and is not so much a labyrinth as a fortress.

This is not to claim it is easy; the fortress is formidable and impressive.
As the four volumes appeared (1924–28), reviewers received them with
more intense wonder and bafflement than had greeted *The Good Soldier*.
'A strange erotic land inhabited principally by sexual monomaniacs',
cried one; 'unclean frauds', another; and a third: 'a nightmare in a
lunatic asylum'. Some thought they recognised in it Ford's own 'anger'
and 'distemper', a reaction that soon for others became a recognition
of the painful emotions it aroused in the reader, and ultimately a

realisation that the agonised involvement of the reader was intentional, a result of Ford's dramatic method designed to wound the consciousness. 'It may be questioned', one wrote, 'whether fiction has any right to make one suffer so much', and thought Ford himself suffered 'from a touch of inhumanity'. Edwin Muir claimed that Ford's insight was not equal to his method: 'Mr Ford has never seized the reality behind the mask' and 'is neither a profound nor a subtle psychologist'. Muir sensed chaos in the novel rather than pain. But L. P. Hartley, in the most perceptive contemporary review, observed what he called 'the pointillism' of Ford's method, 'in which each moment is like a re-birth, a re-awakening to pain and perplexity', a phrase that aptly describes Ford's ability to capture the impression of immediacy.

After the publication of the Knopf omnibus volume in 1950, a dialogue developed between those who championed Ford and hailed the revival and those who qualified and doubted. A few, taking their cue from Robie Macauley's appreciative, sensitive introduction to the Knopf edition, began to try to comprehend and evaluate, to go beyond the book's emotional impact and seek its meaning and importance.

Variously labelled chronicle, fairy tale, allegory, saga, epic, and, more recently, comedy and a modern paradigm of ancient myth and ritual, *Parade's End* has proven that no one label accurately describes its fusion of the expansive and panoramic view with the intensive and dramatic, the affair of a small circle with the crumbling of a civilization. Critical and scholarly investigation from Walter Allen (1946) and Macauley to Andreach and Huntley (1970) has basically agreed on the lines of the novel's structure and the progress of Christopher Tietjens, from his valiant holding on to the values he cherishes to his severe suffering at home and in war and finally to his relinquishment of the past and his reaffirmation. In what almost seems a planned critical progression, the novel has been read as social criticism, psychological case study, political allegory, and pagan-Christian-Dantean myth. Christopher is the last Tory, the gentleman of honour, the limited hero, Adam, the Christ-bearer, the archetypal quester in a journey through hell moving from sin to redemption, and, of course, Ford in disguise, maybe with Mark as his other self. Sylvia is the neurotic society lady, the destroyer, the bitch-*manquée*, the ur-bitch, the white goddess, the twentieth-century Astarte. Valentine is the intellectual, the preserver, Eve, a contemporary Diana and Beatrice. The lists are incomplete, but they suggest the increasingly expanding view of the novel offered by a variety of critical appoaches.

If a relatively consistent, multi-levelled interpretation is emerging, judgements on the novel's artistic excellence differ. Few critics question that *Parade's End* is a remarkable performance, but for some it is a marred masterpiece or only a partial one. Formal critics tend to accept, sometimes reluctantly, *The Good Soldier* as the greater novel; sociological and myth critics tend to prefer *Parade's End*, though it is a sociological critic, John McCormick, who concludes (wrongly, I think) that it is 'a minor effort' because 'Ford was defeated by his attempt to marry social conservatism to technical experiment'. Meixner argues that *Some Do Not* is the finest novel of the series, that it actually says 'all that Ford had to say—about his people and his theme'. The other volumes betray a decline in Ford's creative powers and 'have the unfortunate tendency to leak away in the mind of the reader the impact of the characters who live with such vitality and excitement in the first volume'.

What worries most critics is whether or not *Last Post*,[1] the final volume, is an integral part of the series. Some believe it is sentimental and superfluous and that the Tietjens novels achieve coherence and wholeness without the 'happy' ending. Greene calls it unqualifiedly a disaster and omits it from the Bodley Head edition. If votes decided such matters, however, *Last Post* would be qualifiedly included, since most critics are convinced the series is incomplete without it, and not only for reasons of finishing the thematic and symbolic structure. Ford himself seemed to prefer to leave Tietjens dancing elephant-like through the debris of the past, and yet it can be argued that he also realised the last post is better if sounded and the future actually faced. In any event, the decision in favour of a humble rural existence is inevitable for Tietjens, since the war had neither killed nor destroyed him, and it is fitting that we see him, distraught and resolved, standing before the dying Mark and awaiting the birth of his son, the new Chrissie. Despite the allusiveness, the langour, the dilution of effect evident in *Last Post*, Ford maintains the integrity of Tietjens' character.

Ford's final novels (1928–36) have received little critical attention, except possibly for *The Rash Act* and *Henry for Hugh*, which have the attraction of being engaging literary oddities. Dealing extensively with American subjects and the contemporary trials of double heroes, the late

[1] Published in the United States under the title *The Last Post* (1928), and so titled in Knopf's 1950 *Parade's End* volume.

novels sometimes read like parodies of Hemingway, Sherwood Anderson and Ford himself. At the same time, in them Ford is attempting new directions, perhaps, as Wiley suggests, seeking a new myth to exemplify post-war life. Although at their best they are interesting failures suffering from creative fatigue, they seem deserving of more attention.

We need in addition further study of Ford as critic, both of literature and art, as essayist and as poet: Kenner's essay, first appearing in this volume, being almost the only knowledgeable discussion of Ford as poet and his relation to Pound and Eliot. Much of value remains to be said of Ford as stylist and rhetorician, in both his fiction and non-fiction. We need to know more of his temperamental, intellectual and Catholic (or moral and religious) responses to his Pre-Raphaelite and Victorian heritage in which he was trained and to the twentieth-century innovations he adopted. We have not yet explored all of Ford's sexual insights and the ways they affected his understanding of human nature and found expression in his work. Finally, but not to exhaust the possibilities, we need to define more exactly Ford's use of the comic and the comic forms, especially in the way he often juggles the comic lines so closely to the tragic and painful, and the way he uses comedy as an instrument of vision and artistic self-control.

Currently critics differ as to whether posterity will finally claim *The Good Soldier* and the Tietjens series, or the book on Conrad, or some of the reminiscences like *Return to Yesterday* or *It Was the Nightingale*, or all of these, along with a few poems like 'On Heaven', 'To All the Dead', and 'Antwerp'. Posterity will quite rightly make its own choices, maybe even for the currently neglected testaments of faith, *Provence* and *Great Trade Route*. In the meantime, Ford requires a special effort of the critical imagination. He keeps evading us. All the insight and palaver of current criticism, all the machinery and abracadabra of current research, as valuable as much of it is, has fallen short of achieving really useful definition and appreciation. 'He is at the moment', Richard Foster writes, 'a kind of submerged leviathan, discernible only as an airy spout above a vague, vast ground of surrounding shadow.'[1] Ford, it seems, still resists literal and direct explication. Like his contemporaries seeking to explain his personality, we will probably have to resort to the accuracy of metaphor in order to define and appreciate the complexities and contradictions Ford and his work offer us.   R. A. CASSELL

[1] *Critique*, VII (1965) p.90.

Chronology

(Marginal date indicates actual year of publication; date on title page, If different, follows title.)

1873   Dec 17: Ford Hermann Hueffer born at Merton in Surrey to Francis Hueffer, music critic of the London *Times*, and Catherine Brown Hueffer, daughter of Ford Madox Brown. Shortly after his birth, family moves to London.

1881   Attends Praetoria House, a boarding school for boys in Folkestone.

1889   After father's death, moves with mother and younger brother Oliver to Ford Madox Brown's home. Leaves Praetoria House and becomes for about a year a day-boy at University College School, studying music.

1891   In Paris, baptised a Catholic, assuming as his Christian name: Joseph Leopold Ford Hermann Madox Hueffer. Publishes first poem in *The Torch*, an anarchist journal printed by his Rossetti cousins. *The Brown Owl* (1892; first published book, a fairy story).

1892   *The Feather* (fairy story) and *The Shifting of the Fire* (his first novel).

1893   *The Questions at the Well* (poems under pseudonym of Fenil Haig).

1894   Elopes with Elsie Martindale. Lives near Romney Marsh in Kent. *The Queen Who Flew* (fairy tale).

1896   Moves to Pent Farm, near Portling and Saudling Junction. *Ford Madox Brown: A Record of His Life and Work.*

1898   Moves to Limpsfield in Surrey, near Edward Garnett, who introduces him to Stephen Crane, Galsworthy, Hudson and Conrad. Autumn: he and Conrad agree to collaborate. Leasing

Pent Farm to the Conrads, moves to a cottage at Aldington, near Romney Marsh.

1900　Summer: with Conrads in Belgium for six weeks. *Poems for Pictures* and *The Cinque Ports: A Historical and Descriptive Record.*

1901　Moves to 'The Bungalow' at Winchelsea and begins acquaintance with James, Wells and Arthur Marwood. *The Inheritors,* the first collaborative novel, is published in London and New York.

1902　*Rossetti: A Critical Essay on his Art.*

1903　*Romance,* the second collaborative novel. Becomes ill with an intense depression. For the next three years 'of uninterrupted mental agony' he often visits the Continent, mostly Germany, seeking a cure.

1905　*The Benefactor* (novel); *Hans Holbein the Younger: A Critical Monograph*; *The Soul of London,* which is highly praised, boosting his self-confidence, though he lives with his doctor.

1906　July to Oct: lecture trip to New York. *The Fifth Queen* (novel); *The Heart of the Country*; *Christina's Fairy Book* (fairy tales written for his daughter).

1907　Moves to 84 Holland Park Avenue, which becomes the office for *The English Review.* Mrs Hueffer, after a major operation, moves with children to her property at Aldington. *Privy Seal* (novel); *From Inland and Other Poems*; *An English Girl* (novel); *The Pre-Raphaelite Brotherhood: A Critical Monograph*; *The Spirit of the People: An Analysis of the English Mind*; *The Soul of London, The Heart of the Country,* and *The Spirit of the People* published in America in single volume under title *England and the English.*

1908　Plans *The English Review* with Arthur Marwood and edits first issue (Dec). Meets Violet Hunt. *The Fifth Queen Crowned* and *Mr Apollo* (novels).

1909　Mrs Hueffer begins divorce proceedings. *The 'Half-Moon'* (novel).

1910　After Mrs Hueffer withdraws divorce, spends ten days in jail in protest against restitution of conjugal rights decree. Feb: edits his last issue of *The English Review* and moves with Violet Hunt to her home, South Lodge. *A Call* (novel); *Songs from London* (poems); *The Portrait* (novel).

1911   'Divorce' and 'marriage' with Violet Hunt in Giessen. *Ancient Lights and Certain New Reflections* (memoirs published in America under title *Memories and Impressions*); *The Simple Life Limited* (novel under pseudonym Daniel Chaucer); *Ladies Whose Bright Eyes* (novel); *The Critical Attitude* (a collection of his essays from *The English Review*).

1912   *High Germany: Eleven Sets of Verse* (1911); *The Panel: A Sheer Comedy* (novel published in America in 1913 under title *Ring for Nancy*); *The New Humpty-Dumpty* (second novel under Daniel Chaucer pseudonym).

1913   Mrs Hueffer's successful libel suit against *The Throne*. Dec 17: begins *The Good Soldier*. *This Monstrous Regiment of Women* (pamphlet); *Mr Fleight* (novel); *The Young Lovell* (novel); *The Desirable Alien* (sketches of Germany in collaboration with Violet Hunt).

1914   *Collected Poems*; *Henry James: A Critical Study* (1913; published in America in 1915).

1915   July: commissioned 2nd lieutenant, Welsh Regiment. *The Good Soldier*; *Antwerp* (poems); *When Blood is Their Argument* and *Between St Denis and St George* (for C. F. G. Masterman's government propaganda office). *Zeppelin Nights: A London Entertainment* (1916; stories and sketches in collaboration with Violet Hunt).

1916   In Wales, Rouen and at the front lines. Oct: in Wales suffering from shell-shock, but called back to France near the end of Nov. His lungs give out and by Dec is in a Rouen hospital.

1918   Staff job inspecting and training troops, but towards end of year is sent to front again. *'On Heaven' and Poems Written on Active Service*.

1919   Relinquishes commission on account of ill health and is discharged. Final break with Violet Hunt; changes name legally to Ford Madox Ford; by May is living with Stella Bowen, an Australian artist, at 'Red Ford' in West Sussex.

1921   *Thus to Revisit* (memoirs) and *A House* (poetic drama), the last titles to appear under Hueffer name.

1922   Nov: self-exile from England, returning only for short visits; with Stella Bowen to Paris and Cap Ferrat.

1923   *The Marsden Case* (novel); *Women and Men* (pamphlet); and *Mr Bosphorus and the Muses* (poem).

1924   In Paris, edits *The Transatlantic Review*, Jan to Dec, when it ceases publication. *The Nature of A Crime* (short novel written with Conrad during their collaboration); *Joseph Conrad: A Personal Remembrance*; *Some Do Not* (first novel of Tietjens tetralogy).

1925   *No More Parades* (the second Tietjens novel).

1926   Lecture trip to New York. *A Mirror to France* (essays); *A Man Could Stand Up* (the third Tietjens novel).

1927   *New Poems*; *New York Essays*; *New York is Not America* (essays).

1928   He and Stella Bowen agree to separate. *Last Post* (the final Tietjens novel, titled *The Last Post* in American edition); *A Little Less Than Gods* (novel).

1929   Begins association with Janice Biala, an artist. For the next several years they live in southern France and New York, with some extensive trips through western Europe. *No Enemy: A Tale of Reconstruction* (semi-autobiographical fiction) and *The English Novel*.

1931   *Return to Yesterday* (autobiography) and *When the Wicked Man* (novel, published in England in 1932).

1933   *The Rash Act* (novel) and *It Was the Nightingale* (autobiography).

1934   *Henry for Hugh* (novel, sequel to *The Rash Act*).

1935   *Provence: From Minstrels to the Machine* (personal, sociological essay); a revised edition of *Ladies Whose Bright Eyes*.

1936   *Vive le Roy* (the final novel) and a new edition of *Collected Poems*.

1937   *Portraits from Life* (literary criticism; published in England under title *Mightier Than the Sword*, 1938); *Great Trade Route* (personal, sociological essay). Aug: begins year of lecturing and writing at Olivet College, Michigan, which awards him a Doctor of Letters.

1938   *The March of Literature from Confucius' Day to Our Own* (published in England in 1939).

1939   Lecturing in the United States. May: returns to France. 26 June: dies of heart failure in Deauville, France. Buried in the English cemetery, Deauville.

EZRA POUND

Ford Madox Ford (1939)

THERE passed from us this June a very gallant combatant for those things of the mind and of letters which have been in our time too little prized. There passed a man who took in his time more punishment of one sort and another than I have seen meted to anyone else. For the ten years before I got to England there would seem to have been no one but Ford who held that French clarity and simplicity in the writing of English verse and prose were of immense importance as in contrast to the use of a stilted traditional dialect, a 'language of verse' unused in the actual talk of the people, even of 'the best people,' for the expression of reality and emotion.

In 1908 London was full of 'gargoyles', of poets, that is, with high reputation, most of whose work has gone since into the discard. At that time, and in the few years preceding, there appeared without notice various fasciculae which one can still, surprisingly, read and they were not designed for mouthing, for the 'rolling out' of 'ohs'. They weren't what people were looking for as the prolongation of Victoria's glory. They weren't, that is, 'intense' in the then sense of the word.

The justification or programme of such writing was finally (about 1913) set down in one of the best essays (preface) that Ford ever wrote.

It advocated the prose value of verse-writing, and it, along with his verse, had more in it for my generation than all the retchings (most worthily) after 'quantity' (i.e., quantitative metric) of the late Laureate Robert Bridges or the useful, but monotonous, in their day unduly neglected, as more recently unduly touted, metrical labours of G. Manley Hopkins.

I have put it down as personal debt to my forerunners that I have had five, and only five, useful criticisms of my writing in my lifetime, one from Yeats, one from Bridges, one from Thomas Hardy, a recent one from a Roman Archbishop and one from Ford, and that last the most vital, or at any rate on par with Hardy's.

That Ford was almost an *halluciné* few of his intimates can doubt. He felt until it paralysed his efficient action, he saw quite distinctly the Venus immortal crossing the tram tracks. He inveighed against Yeats' lack of emotion as, for him, proved by Yeats' so great competence in making literary use of emotion.

And he felt the errors of contemporary style to the point of rolling (physically, and if you look at it as a mere superficial snob, ridiculously) on the floor of his temporary quarters in Giessen when my third volume displayed me trapped, fly-papered, gummed and strapped down in a jejune provincial effort to learn, *mehercule*, the stilted language that then passed for 'good English' in the arthritic milieu that held control of the respected British critical circles, Newbolt, the backwash of Lionel Johnson, Fred Manning, the Quarterlies and the rest of 'em.

And that roll saved me at least two years, perhaps more. It sent me back to my own proper effort, namely, toward using the living tongue (with younger men after me), though none of us has found a more natural language than Ford did.

This is a dimension of poetry. It is, magari, an Homeric dimension, for of Homer there are at least two dimensions apart from the surge and thunder. Apart from narrative sense and the main constructive, there is this to be said of Homer, that never can you read half a page without finding melodic invention, still fresh, and that you can hear the actual voices, as of the old men speaking in the course of the phrases.

It is for this latter quality that Ford's poetry is of high importance, both in itself and for its effect on all the best subsequent work of his time. Let no young snob forget this.

I propose to bury him in the order of merits as I think he himself understood them, first for an actual example in the writing of poetry; secondly, for those same merits more fully shown in his prose, and thirdly, for the critical acumen which was implicit in his finding these merits.

As to his prose, you can apply to it a good deal that he wrote in praise of Hudson (rightly) and of Conrad, I think with a bias toward generosity that in parts defeats its critical applicability. It lay so natural on the page that one didn't notice it. I read an historical novel at sea in 1906 without noting the name of the author. A scene at Henry VIIIth's court stayed depicted in my memory and I found years later that Ford had written it.

I wanted for private purposes to make a note on a point raised in *Ancient Lights*; I thought it would go on the back of an envelope, and found to my young surprise that I couldn't make the note in fewer words than those on Ford's actual page. That set me thinking. I did not in those days care about prose. If 'prose' meant anything to me, it meant Tacitus (as seen by Mackail), a damned dangerous model for a young man in those days or these days in England, though I don't regret it; one never knows enough about anything. Start with Tacitus and be cured by Flaubert via Ford, or start with Ford or Maupassant and be girt up by Tacitus, after fifty it is *kif, kif,* all one. But a man is a pig not to be grateful to both sides.

Until the arrival of such 'uncomfortables' as Wyndham Lewis, the distressful D. H. Lawrence, D. Goldring, G. Cannan, etc., I think Ford had no one to play with. The elder generation loathed him, or at any rate such cross-section of it as I encountered. He disturbed 'em, he took Dagon by the beard, publicly. And he founded the greatest Little Review or pre-Little Review of our time. From 1908 to 1910 he gathered into one fasciculus the work of Hardy, H. James, Hudson, Conrad, C. Graham, Anatole France, the great old-stagers, the most competent of that wholly unpleasant decade, Bennett, Wells, and, I think, even Galsworthy.

And he got all the first-rate and high second-raters of my own decade, W. Lewis, D. H. Lawrence (made by Ford, dug out of a board school in Croydon), Cannan, Walpole, etc. (Eliot was not yet on the scene).

The inner story of that review and the treatment of Ford by its obtainers is a blot on London's history that time will not remove, though, of course, it will become invisible in the perspective of years.

As critic he was perhaps wrecked by his wholly unpolitic generosity. In fact, if he merits an epithet above all others, it would be 'The Unpolitic'. Despite all his own interests, despite all the hard-boiled and half-baked vanities of all the various lots of us, he kept on discovering merit with monotonous regularity.

His own best prose was probably lost, as isolated chapters in un-achieved and too-quickly-issued novels. He persisted in discovering capacities in similar crannies. In one weekly after another he found and indicated the capacities of Mary, Jenny, Willard, Jemimah, Horatio, etc., despite the fact that they all of 'em loathed each other, and could by no stretch of imagination be erected into a compact troop of Fordites supporting each other and moving on the citadels of publication.

And that career I saw him drag through three countries. He took up the fight for free letters in Paris, he took it up again in New York, where I saw him a fortnight before his death, still talking of meritorious novels, still pitching the tale of unknown men who had written the *histoire morale contemporaine* truthfully and without trumpets, told this or that phase of America as seen from the farm or the boiler-works, as he had before wanted young England to see young England from London, from Sussex.

And of all the durable pages he wrote (for despite the fluff, despite the apparently aimless meander of many of 'em, he did write durable pages) there is nothing that more registers the fact of our day than the two portraits in the, alas, never-finished *Women and Men* (Three Mountains Press, 1923), Meary Walker and 'T.'[1]

SOURCE: *Homage to Ford Madox Ford*, New Directions, no. 7 (1942

NOTE

1. [*Editor's note*] Harvey in his bibliography (p. 56) notes that 'Pound's obituary assumes, apparently wrongly, that *Women and Men* was never finished'.

EDWARD CRANKSHAW

The Ford Case (1948)

IT is characteristic of the sad story of Ford Madox Ford that even now, nine years after his death, he is more often remembered by his life than by his work. This would not have surprised him. Throughout most of his career he had to watch his contemporaries not only engrossing themselves in his private affairs, but also attributing to his work undesirable qualities said to be found in the man. The most agonisedly reticent of human beings, there was nothing he could do to stop it. His silences provoked still wilder imaginings; his forlorn attempts to throw a smoke-screen round himself produced through the distorting haze, the apparition of a monster, like a pink elephant, absurd, bizarre, immense. And the more, once committed to the public gaze, he struggled to produce a fictitious personality, the more extravagantly coloured the world's image of him became. When at last he simply went away and was forgotten, his work was forgotten too.

He died three months before the outbreak of war, at Deauville, on the journey from America to Provence. Two friends, one of them English, attended the funeral of the man who had once been almost suffocated by the weight of his friends and who throughout his life had poured out time and energy, as well as the practical wisdom he so completely failed to apply to his own affairs, for the unstinted benefit of any new writer of any promise whatsoever who cared to apply. Even this death in tawdry exile was not the end. Any other man could have counted on resting in peace on the Normandy cliffs among the acres of rusting metal crosses and hotly glittering glass domes of the municipal cemetery. But not Ford. . . . Before the year was out his grave was a site for German anti-aircraft guns protecting an advanced dive-bomber station. It has not yet been re-visited. The whole of Ford's life is in the story of his death and burial, separated from England by

the breadth of the sea, in surroundings representing everything he held
detestable, unhonoured.

Of all men he held most firmly to the idea that an artist's private life
belongs to him and to nobody else. This was not a consequence of his
own humiliations; it was a settled principle. In one of his earliest books,
a small monograph on Rossetti, he says at the outset:

> 'Again, the most profitable method of criticism is that of paying attention to
> a man's work. . . . The artist should be allowed to live out his life in peace.
> If he is not, if the censor of manners must for the public good be called
> in to say: "This man was a good citizen and saved money; this a Bohemian
> who worked after supper", our view of his art becomes generally less clear.'

It is time someone said this for Ford.

But the muddles of his own private life continue to pursue him after
death. At the very moment when the four novels of the first World
War (*Some Do Not . . ., A Man Could Stand Up, No More Parades* and
Last Post), at the very moment when these volumes reappear as
Penguins, offering a new generation which is not interested in Miss Hunt
the chance to rediscover a neglected master for itself, Mr Goldring
comes forward [in *The Last Pre-Raphaelite*] with a discussion of the
celebrated private life, and the whole sad, dreary business starts up
again. Certainly the new generation stumbling across *Some Do Not . . .*
will want to know what possessed its parents to leave out of considera-
tion the work of so consummate an artist. The possible justification for
Mr Goldring's book is that it offers part of the answer to that question.
On the other hand it might have been better had Ford's own expressed
wish for no biography been respected, at any rate until all concerned
are dead. For it is really impossible to do justice to Ford without wound-
ing others. It is probably impossible to do justice to Ford in any case.
And when it comes to the Tietjens novels Mr R. A. Scott-James' warm
and eloquent little introduction is all that is really required to 'place'
them.

It is necessary to touch on this matter because Mr Goldring's book
is about little else. Mr Goldring was Ford's assistant in the office of *The
English Review*, and saw little of his subject in his latter years, which, in
a way, were the happiest of Ford's life. His book is offered as an act of
piety; but there is only one way to make up for the wrongs done to
a dead writer in his lifetime, and that is to clear the ground about his

work. This Mr Goldring does not do. Instead he gives us the image of the man who so bewildered his contemporaries that they rejected him. One day there will emerge from the tangle of misapprehensions the figure of a man whose whole life was his work—as a poet virtually unknown, as a prophet ignored, as a novelist neglected—and in his unending struggle to persuade society to recognise the artist. In this struggle he threw all his energies into the causes of others, forgetting to count in his own magnificent achievement. But that will remain.

The important truth about Ford as a man is that he was afflicted with an ungovernable integrity. The great public scandals of the Third Republic, all of which contributed to the break-down of France, were commonly taken by censorious Anglo-Saxons as proof of a peculiar corruption. Corruption certainly existed as a normal component of human society. But corruption exists elsewhere without provoking moral crises intense enough to split a modern state from top to bottom. What caused the scandals was not the corruption but the ungovernable integrity of certain Frenchmen, who, like Clemenceau in the Dreyfus case, found it intolerable that wrong should be allowed to strangle right, even if the publishing of a secret crime meant the disruption of France and the dishonouring of her army. The absence of a Dreyfus case from the annals of recent British history is not a reflection of our national integrity, but of what we like to call our sense of proportion. This sense of proportion Ford, with the French incorruptibles, totally lacked. Add to this deficiency, or quality, an exacerbated sensibility caused by the lack of several outer skins, wall it round with a studied and sometimes offensive manner (excusable only in the invulnerable, who would have no use for it), and by the misleadingly assertive glitter of a bogus personality projected to distract the eye from uncertainty within, and you have the essentials of the great Ford mystery, or muddle, which is important only in so far as it is reflected in Ford's work (his chief characters, for example, also lack a sense of proportion, or common sense). No child could have been taken in by Ford; but, to his own undoing, many adults were.

The remarkable aspect of the Ford case is not that the man was misconceived by his contemporaries, but that this misconception was allowed to obscure his manifest gifts. These in any case would have had a hard struggle to make themselves felt, if only because Ford produced his best work at the worst possible time, while his literary 'references' had the worst possible associations for that time. That is to say, in brief, that apart from *The Good Soldier* which appeared in 1914, and was immediately swallowed up by the first German war, his masterpieces did not begin to appear until the publication of *Some Do Not . . .*, in 1924. Ford by that time was already dated as the associate of Henry James and Stephen Crane, who had been dead for several years and who were both then overlaid by later novelists. What is worse, he was known as the friend and collaborator of the early Conrad; and Conrad died in that very year, plunging steeply into temporary oblivion. Thus, although both *The Good Soldier* and the four Tietjens novels were received by diverse critics with the startled and somewhat flurried homage accorded evident masterpieces which are unexpected and cannot easily be placed, nobody at that time wanted to read the sort of book they thought Ford must be writing. The co-author of *Romance* and *The Inheritors*, the adviser of Conrad in his *Nostromo* period, the late editor of *The English Review* and champion of the Vorticists, the gifted dilettante critic and poet who had somehow touched an un-expected summit of accomplishment in the limited field of the historic-al novel, with the astonishing *tour de force* of the *Fifth Queen* and its two successors, the familiar, not-to-be-taken-seriously figure of Edwardian London who had gone off to the war under a cloud and never, apparently, come back—this was not the sort of man to have anything to say to a generation which was gulping Lawrence and Proust and waiting hungrily for Eliot and Joyce. To crown the situation, *Some Do Not . . .* and its successors were largely about the war, and people were not yet prepared to read about the war. When they were so prepared they wanted it neat; the cataclysm to which they owed their disorientation had to be magnified into a monstrous negation of everything that had ever happened. Ford, intent on showing the Flanders battle as one aspect of contemporary history, did not fulfil this need.

Even those who read him, full of admiration for his talent, were puzzled. All the past of Ford, all Hueffer, in a word, belonged to a ruined epoch; and yet these novels did not belong to that epoch. All the present belonged to Joyce and Proust and Ezra Pound, whom he advertised loudly as he had once advertised Conrad and James; but they were not in these novels. All the future belonged to the young, the tongue-tied generation of Hemingway, the dumb ox, whom Ford himself caught and bullied into articulateness. But these novels were not dumb. They were neither past nor present nor future, as these abstractions were so sympathetically defined by Ford himself. Evidently, then, he was a failure, one of those artists of marked talent who never make the grade, a sort of forerunner, a Baptist of *Les Deux Magots*. And so effectively did this selfless genius preach the supremacy of his chosen swans, or geese, that it never occured to anyone that all the time he was tenaciously and stubbornly pursuing a line of his own, not faltering somewhat timidly in the footsteps of Conrad, James, Lawrence, Proust, Joyce, Hemingway, or what have you. The artist and the connoisseur of the new in art are rarely found in one person; in Ford, though they rarely met, they existed side by side, and the reputation of the one was killed by the reputation of the other. 'Watch Conrad!' he would murmur confidentially, gasping for breath between the syllables. 'Watch Lawrence—Watch Béhaine—Watch Joyce—Watch Faulkner—Watch Greenc. . . . !' But never: 'Watch me!' Indeed, driven by what compulsion, he sought persistently to divert attention from his own work as a novelist by parading himself as a cook, a horticulturalist, a composer of symphonies at the age of sixteen. His own work as a novelist, nevertheless, though little known to the general reader and ignored by the critic and the public assessor of tendencies and trends, has, like the air we breathe, quietly found its way, either directly or through others, into the work of many of the best contemporary writers. So that when he opens the latest offering of Mr Greene, *The Heart of the Matter*, the first thing that strikes the attentive reader is the unseen presence of Ford.

How that presence makes itself felt, or what, in a word, Ford's contribution to the English novel really amounts to, is far from easy to define. He was not a breaker of new ground in the normal sense of that image. Rather, he was the supreme cultivator. If he had a theory of the novel it was an entirely commonsense theory. Indeed, poetically, all the commonsense missing from Ford's transactions as a member of society went into his approach to art, to literature. For what, above all, he gave was, precisely, a sense of proportion. He combined, for example, a rigid structure with extreme flexibility and range of expression. The range and flexibility to which he aspired had to be firmly anchored. Anchorage could be supplied only by the clearest and strictest terms of references. The precision of his constructions was not arbitrary; it arose from the precision of his conceptions. Thus, *The Good Soldier*, the most perfect of his novels, is in every way a text-book novel; but it is not what is understood by a novelist's novel. The precision of the machining, the high polish of the surface of this extraordinary narrative, which plumbs the obscurest chambers of the human soul with about as much fuss as a black boy diving for pennies, is simply a reflection of the articulation of the story, which cannot be analysed apart from the story. Here the novel seems to grow as, in Conrad's word, the style of Hudson grew, 'like the green grass'. It is all invention, and yet, in the words of Miss Rebecca West, 'behind it is a force of passion which so sustains the story in its flight that never once does it appear as the work of man's invention'.

Nowadays almost the last repository of good fiction is the detective story. This may distress, but need not surprise. The writer, the artist of any kind, is only free when he is quite sure of his subject, whether it is a Madonna or a murder. Given that fixed point, that anchorage, he can range where he likes. The detective novel has such an anchorage; a fixed, a static point, upon which all the action must converge, however remote and peripheral; 'Who did it?' This centripetal structure is the foundation of all the novels of Ford, in which all the actions of all the characters bear down on a single, fixed point. His plots, that is to say, turn not upon what the hero does but upon what happens to him as a result of what he does. There is nothing revolutionary in this approach. Euripides and Shakespeare both used it. But in the novel it had no place until Henry James and, above all, Conrad developed it as the supreme method, the only method, indeed, for getting the last ounce of meaning from a given spiritual crisis. Ford, taking over from them (and having a great deal to do with the development of Conrad's architectonics so splendidly revealed in *Chance* and *Under Western Eyes*), thus was far from inventing the centripetal construction, as opposed to the centrifugal construction (if you can call it that), instinctively resorted to by past novelists of the English tradition, including some distinguished foreigners, such as Tolstoi himself. But he developed it past belief, and in two distinct aspects. It is this development which makes itself felt in much of the most accomplished fiction of to-day, as, for example, in the work of Mr Greene.

James and Conrad, revolting in their various ways against the loose panoramic construction with its great weakness of diffusion and its multiplicity of offshoots leading nowhere, sought to focus the reader's attention on a central crisis which would colour the mood of the book throughout and towards which all the action would point. Conrad himself expressed this preoccupation when introducing Marlow in *The Heart of Darkness*:

'To him the meaning of an episode was not inside like a kernel but outside, enveloping the tale which brought it out only as a glow brings out a haze, in the likeness of one of those misty halos that sometimes are made visible by the spectral illumination of moonshine.' The whole narrative apparatus of Conrad, including Marlow himself, is called up to answer this very preoccupation, which was shared, in rather different terms, by James. These two, intent on focussing all their gifts on the central affair, or crisis, were driven to various forms of isolation. James isolated his characters from humdrum society by ignoring that society; Conrad, with a far wider range of experience and finding his characters in many walks of life, still isolated his central affair by steeping his stories, even *The Secret Agent*, in a strong romantic dye. Both, that is to say, in achieving concentration, unity, and perfectly expressive form, abandoned more or less what had hitherto been the exclusive field of the novel: portrayal of the life and manners of society. They exalted the novel for the first time in English to the level of the highest art by forcing certain aspects of it, at the expense of others, in a hot-house temperature.

But Ford, sharing completely the ideals of Conrad and James, was nevertheless equally concerned with the novel as a mirror of society. In his eyes the aim of the novelist must be to illuminate the human heart in terms of contemporary experience. This purpose he achieved by turning the very methods perfected by his seniors as instruments of exclusion into a gigantic apparatus of inclusion, and without sacrificing any of their effectiveness in the task for which they were evolved. Thus, in the Tietjens novels, and subject only to the limitations of his genius, he combined the intensiveness of the new school with the extensiveness of the old masters.

On the one hand, by taking the reader straight to the heart of the matter, the permanent crisis arising from what Tietjens had done (his marriage with Sylvia and his refusal to divorce her for adultery), by allowing the past to appear only in terms of the present, thus automatically excluding everything that lacks a direct bearing on the present (i.e., the subject), by allowing no character to appear or to speak except in so far as he contributes to the Tietjens crisis and by never for a moment letting the reader forget that crisis (the stories of Sylvia, Mark and Valentine being in no way digressions but rather inward-pointing arrows)—by attending to all this, he achieved a concentration and unity equal to that achieved by Conrad in *Chance*. Indeed, his strategy was identical with Conrad's though his tactics are entirely individual.

On the other hand, by standing his chief character in the very centre of contemporary life, instead of well off-centre (which is the normal position for the hero in the novels of Conrad and James and other novelists of the human spirit), by bringing into his orbit wave after wave of common humanity from all ranks and all stations, and always converging on the centre—indeed, pulled towards the centre, Tietjens, as the tides are pulled towards the moon; by, above all, abjuring lay figures and giving full value to every subsidiary character, from the unseen banker's son who tries to ruin Tietjens with an R.D. cheque, to 09 Morgan who stumbles into a dug-out to die all over Tietjens' feet (absolutely full value; there is not an atom of difference between the treatment of Tietjens in four volumes and 09 Morgan in scattered lines) —by attending to all this, Ford is able to weave his chief characters into the fabric of society as a whole and thus achieve the panoramic sweep of the traditionalists.

This combination, this synthesis of opposed developments in the novel, is one of the things we have in mind when speaking of the presence of Ford in the work of his more interesting successors. It has to do with the structure and therefore the content and expressiveness of the novel as a whole. The other thing has to do with the structure, the content and expressiveness of the individual scene, or paragraph, or sentence. For just as in the architecture of the novel every scene, every action, every character, is subordinated to the laws of the moon, so, in the detail, every paragraph, every sentence, every word shows the same subordination. It is not simply that there are no purple patches; there is scarcely a quotable sentence throughout the four Tietjens novels. And yet every sentence is finished. In memory these novels are rich in palpable impressions of things seen; in fact there is scarcely a single description of a scene or even a mood. The impressions take shape and group themselves as one reads by means of a word here, a phrase there, as the story requires. But what one is reading is always the story. This is more than the subordination of impressions to a central theme, as in Conrad and James; it is the atomisation of life and its recreation by rearrangement of minute components—and with the uninhibited use of every conceivable technical device in the novelist's armoury.

Thus beneath the smooth surface, which does not look like invention, lies the most arduous and finished experimentation. *The Good Soldier*, the four Tietjens novels, and their successors, have none of the disarming floundering and lack of balance which we associate with experimentation; they have the faultless lucidity of the habitual. It would be truer to call them revolutionary prototypes than experiments; all the tears and striving lie behind them. It is unfortunate for the original artist if his work is not immediately recognisable as such. Because a concealed novelty strikes obscurely, sounding inexplicable overtones of unease. This happened to Ford, who was rejected not, as so many thought, because he had nothing new to say, but because he had too much and with new accents which most readers took for the old.

SOURCE: *National Review*, CXXXI (1948).

MORTON DAUWEN ZABEL

The Last Pre-Raphaelite
(1949, 1956)

THE rough justice and grim fortune that dealt unsparingly with Ford
Madox Ford during his more than forty years of authorship pursued
him down to the time of his death in France in 1939, and seem intent
on pursuing him even yet. Today all, or nearly all, of his eighty or
more books are out of print. He still figures rarely, if at all, among the
century's ranking novelists. Ignored or slighted in later years in his own
country, he received there, on dying, the official obloquy and grudging
sarcasm of the obituarists of what in his day he had stubbornly resisted,
'the Establishment'. (The only decent memorial notice that seems to
have appeared in London was a tribute by Graham Greene in *The
Spectator*.) France and America gave him such success as he finally came
by in the last twenty years of his long career, but after serving literature
for half a century in three countries, his only official honor was a degree
from Olivet College, Michigan, of which he was gratefully proud.
The irony of this curiously baffled career persists even in the memoir
and single book-length study of Ford which has thus far appeared—
that of his one-time assistant on *The English Review*, Douglas Goldring,
which was called *The Last Pre-Raphaelite* when it appeared in London
in 1948 and which was titled, with a similar accent of ironic pathos,
Trained for Genius when it was published in New York a year later.

Much as he exploited his Pre-Raphaelite ancestry and apprenticeship,
Ford knew the liability that glamorous inheritance had laid on him. He
was 'trained for genius' all too overpoweringly. It took him a large part
of his life to find his real work and bearings as a writer. A sense of in-
security in his revered vocation never wholly left him. But it will be
unfortunate if these titles mislead Mr Goldring's readers. He was
Ford's staunchest English friend; he writes with a mixture of amused
realism and stubborn respect about the man he has always considered
his literary guide and master; and he has never forgotten the debt he

owed Ford for being taken on, at twenty-one in 1908, as sub-editor of *The English Review*, thus gaining privileged access to the highest conclaves of modern English authorship. The book is, in fact, the second of Mr Goldring's tributes to Ford. In 1943 he published in London a memoir called *South Lodge*. Its pages are not incorporated in the later volume, which is a pity, for *South Lodge* is a better book than *Trained for Genius*—a vivid evocation of the part of Ford's history Mr Goldring knew at first hand, with a brilliant picture of literary and social London on the eve of 1914, a sound account of Ford's successes and miseries in that remote era, and a haunting portrait of Violet Hunt, that embattled 'woman who did', from her disastrous entry into Ford's life until she died at eighty, alone, unforgetting, deranged, among her houseful of trophies, while the bombs of 1942 provided 'the orchestral thunder of a dying age'.

Mr Goldring's will not be the last word on Ford. His biography is without exact scholarship, and his criticism, while roughly valid, yields to defensive polemic. Ford made a deathbed request against biographies. His American legatee honored this wish by refusing to cooperate. The Paris years are merely sketched, and the chapter on Ford's American career is completely inadequate, since none of his important friends here were consulted. It is, moreover, a bold biographer who would venture on this task at all. Ford's own accounts of himself were, for all their richness of content, always unreliable and often fantastic: 'impressions of truth' according to their author, congenital lying according to his enemies, incredibly embarrassing, wheezily garrulous even to his friends, with their quagmires of yarn-spinning and stories that never quite agreed twice. Had he really been dandled by Turgenev, had his chair stolen at a concert by Liszt, modeled for Densher in *The Wings of the Dove*, gone to Eton, attended the Sorbonne? The reader could never be sure. And beyond these erratic records lies a muddle of gossip and legend and what a host of ladies had to say about their parts in it—Violet Hunt's *I Have This to Say: The Story of My Flurried Years*, Jean Rhys's *After Leaving Mr McKenzie*, Stella Bowen's *Drawn from Life*, and a cloud of other documents in scandal, defense, and litigation. Ford had a genius for making messes. Even his strokes of fortune—friendship with James, collaboration with Conrad, contacts with Wells, Bennett, and other Edwardian talents, brilliant editorships of *The English Review* and the *Transatlantic*—were

riddled by misunderstanding or mismanagement. His ventures in and
out of marriage became a minor epic of error and tactlessness. Nor does
the case become simpler when his file of eighty books and massive
journalism are tackled. Novels, verse, essays, criticism, memoirs,
biographies, travels, histories, sociology, they range from potboiling
meretriciousness to distinction, the incessant outpourings of a poly-
graph who apparently wrote something every day of his life from
fifteen to sixty-six. Criticism, for understandable reasons, has hardly
begun to make something of this vast bulk of print. (Mr Robie Macauley's perceptive essay in the *Kenyon Review*, Spring 1949, and Mr
Mark Schorer's introduction to the 1951 reprint of *The Good Soldier*,
though they both idealize rather drastically, will perhaps serve as points
of departure for the serious assessment of Ford's achievement that may
eventually arrive.)

The fact is that Ford's aesthetic origins and association served him
both well and badly. They made it impossible for him to live any other
life than that of literature, and to live it whole-souledly and passionately.
They also made it impossible for him ever quite to sell himself to
journalism, propaganda, or profitably slick mass-production like such
comparable polygraphs as Wells and Maugham. They kept him
through five decades a lover of good writing, original talent, authentic
invention. But his dedication to form, style, and the *mot juste*, coupled
with his habit of pontificating, desire to *faire école* at all costs, and
compulsive addiction to paper ('an old man mad about writing'),
likewise kept him writing, prosing, repeating himself, when there was,
very often, little actual substance to work on. Style, technique, manner,
and method were kept grinding away, half the time saying little and
producing what can be, for long and desperate stretches, a garrulously
tiresome parody of his intentions.

The better Ford was not a man spinning literature spiderwise out of
his own entrails. For all his social, political, religious, and personal
inconsistencies, he was a man who lived through and in his age. He
never betrayed what Mr Goldring rightly calls his highest merit, his
unswerving loyalty to 'the Standard of Values' and to the art that
supported that standard when, in a demoralized and violent time, every
other support was likely to fail. He was also a man who, though often
mistaken, pretentious, foolish, or deluded, was never essentially self-
deceived. He knew in his own life the risks, ignominy, and treacheries

of his period. Whenever he drew on his two soundest resources—his instinct of honor, his generous sense of justice—he wrote out of a saving reserve of character. He could locate and trace the problem of honor in history—the Katherine Howard trilogy or *Ladies Whose Bright Eyes*—and find an original means to define it there. He could define it even better in his own age—in *The Good Soldier* and the Tietjens series—the first, as Graham Greene says, 'a study of an averagely good man of a conventional class driven, divided, and destroyed by unconventional passion', the second an 'appalling examination of how private malice goes on during public disaster', both of them to be counted among 'the novels which stand as high as any fiction written since the death of James'. This estimate is high, perhaps, like Mr Goldring's, finally too high, but if it errs it does so on the side of justice.

Traditionalist, *révolté*; Catholic, skeptic; agrarian and internationalist; 'small producer' and restless migrant; democratic, ritual-lover, and iconoclast; fond father, erring husband, harassed lover; loyal to England, to Germany, and to France—he was all these by turns and never fully succeeded in stabilizing or centering his personal or artistic loyalties. He came to reject half his work as 'worthless', wrote remorselessly day after day, found joy elusive and trouble sure, died at last in poverty (though with two hundred manuscripts by young writers in his keeping, recipients of his unflagging care and encouragement), was written off as 'dated' in England, soon forgotten in France, unread even in America. 'But', says Graham Greene, 'I don't suppose failure disturbed him much: he had never really believed in human happiness, his middle life had been made miserable by passion, and he had come through, with his humour intact, his stock of unreliable anecdotes, the kind of enemies a man ought to have, and a half-belief in a posterity which would care for good writing.' Twice this life of avid human and aesthetic charity, un-self-protective impulse, and serious artistic dedication found the subject that could express its baffled generosity, once in *The Good Soldier*, again in the bitter fortunes of Christopher Tietjens; and in those two books—in the first of them with subtle poignance and studied craftsmanship, in the second with a more acute moral ferocity if, eventually, with a damaging distention of its material —he found the art he had groped toward with such dutiful understudy and painful search, so at last justifying himself as the artist he had always wanted to be, in a craft he held to be 'the noblest to which a man can dedicate himself'.

Mr Goldring presents Ford complete with all his errors and faults, but with his honor intact too, and with what D. H. Lawrence, who owed his debut to Ford and *The English Review* and who could understand Ford's kind of ordeal, called the 'dove-grey kindliness' by which he served literature. 'There was none too much of it left in the world after Ford's departure', adds Mr Goldring, 'which is no doubt one of the reasons why some of us, who knew him, cherish his memory.' For those who didn't know him, Ford left other, less elusive evidence.

He left a record of creative sympathy that refused to rely on vested interests and prejudices but kept itself alert to the risk and independence that ensure the truth of moral insight. He carried over from the aesthetic radicalism of his Victorian sponsors a respect for the nonconformism that enlarges the boundaries of the imagination and of the arts that embody it. He allied himself consistently with the kind of energy that resists stultification by habit or easy success by compromise with standardized taste. He never lost his confidence that the methods of fiction and poetry were still open to new possibilities of invention, style, and discipline. And with this openness to novelty and experiment he joined, with an authority few men of his generation could so effectively define, a sense of the continuity and integrity of a literary tradition: of what Romantic and Victorian art had to offer as a basis of poetic discovery, and of what the novel of Joyce, Hemingway, and their contemporaries had to rely on in the disciplines established by the classic line of Stendhal, Flaubert, Turgenev, James, and Conrad.

The distractions of his personal life, the fitful and erratic impulses of his writing, justified themselves at last in this: that his zeal for innovation was never without its respect for the continuities of craft and discipline; that his susceptibility to untried talent had schooled itself in the discoveries that had proved their worth in the past and had demonstrated there how the tests of art form a constant mediation between past and future in the living ordeal of present truth and sincerity. Ford thus made himself, as novelist and teacher of novelists, a force of balance and compromise between two traditions whose necessary collision in the Twentieth Century he was one of the few to see, as he was one of the few to show, not only in his two real achievements in fiction but in the personal discomfort that made them possible, what their reconciliation imposed on the modern writer as a test of his courage and intelligence. It was logical that Ezra Pound, when he found Ford in the London of 1910, should have singled him out for tribute: 'In a country in love with amateurs, in a country where the incompetent have such beautiful manners, and personalities so fragile and charming, that one cannot bear to injure their feelings by the introduction of competent criticism, it is well that one man should have a vision of perfection and that he should be sick to death and disconsolate because he cannot attain it.'

Ford was never sufficiently blessed to lose either the vision or the dissatisfaction that accompanied it. Among so many books that seem to compromise his commitment and among the private misadventures that continually harassed it, he left two solid achievements and a lifetime's example of unprofitable generosity to testify to his refusal of complacency. It remains the task of his followers to recognize the evidence he left of what that refusal entailed, and, now that the necessary interval of posthumous probation has passed, to respect him for it.

SOURCE: M. D. Zabel, *Craft and Character in Modern Fiction* (1949, 1957).

R. W. LID

Tietjens in Disguise (1964)

'He's an incredible ass. . . .' AN ENGLISH GIRL

IT took Ford over twenty years of writing to find his true subject matter and the individual techniques he needed to handle it. During those laborious twenty years he fell under the varying influences of Turgenev, Flaubert, Conrad, and James. It was not Conrad but James who played the largest role in the development of his art. What Ford learned in collaborating with Conrad was his own—nothing borrowed, nothing imitative. But James presented him with the linked temptations of easily borrowable or easily accessible themes and techniques and style.

> On re-reading this morning, after an interval of perhaps twenty-five years, *The American*, I find that I have introduced, almost exactly as he stands in that book, one of Mr James' characters into one of my own novels, written five years ago. You see, I first read *The American* during a period of my boyhood passed very largely in Paris, and very largely in exactly the same society as that in which Newman himself moved. And having read the book at the same time I really, twenty years after, thought that Valentin de Bellegarde was a young man that I had met somewhere. . . . Yes, indeed, I thought that Valentin was one of my own connections whom I had liked very much. And so I considered myself perfectly justified in lifting his figure, with such adornments and changes as should suit my own purpose, into one of my own novels.[1]

Ford's somewhat belated self-revelation and his less than successful attempt at self-justification are an index of the complex story of his indebtedness to James.

If Count Carlo Canzano, who is modeled on Valentin de Bellegarde, carries some of the authenticity of the Jamesian word into *An English Girl* (1907), it is not because Ford knew the same social world as James (which of course he did not), or because Ford himself had met Canzano on occasion during afternoons-at-home (as he is claiming here), but because Canzano is a thoroughgoing imitation of James.

A trip to America which Ford and his wife took in 1906 was the immediate occasion that suggested *An English Girl*. Ostensibly the novel deals with the 'international theme' in the same way as 'Lady Barberina' and *Portrait of a Lady*: it plays upon the moral and cultural antinomies of two civilizations as, in this case, 'an English girl' becomes involved in the American scene. Actually, the heroine, Eleanor Greville, shares the stage with a hero, the American Don Collar Kelleg, and the novel is more *his* than hers. For into a typical Jamesian situation Ford introduces his own particular heroic fantasy: the deracinated young hero, out of joint with his time, filled with aesthetic idealism and social purpose, but helpless to act. That fantasy is merely a shorthand cipher of Ford's own problem as an artist.

Don and Eleanor are engaged to be married. They have met while studying art under Whistler in a Paris atelier. As the novel opens, they have just learned of the death of Don's father, an American business-man who made his fortune through juggling stocks and manipulating holding companies. Overnight Don becomes 'the richest man in the world', and the position of the couple changes. They can no longer look forward to the simple, retired life of the English family of means. Don assumes 'a portentous identity' in the eyes of the world.

> A voice behind her back uttered:
> 'Oh, I suppose he's come down to see if he won't buy the cathedral.'
> And another:
> 'Oh, he *couldn't* do that, could he? Doesn't it belong to the State or something.'[2]

To Don the inheritance becomes a burden. Society must be repaid for the wrongs committed by his father in amassing such a fortune. ' "Heaven knows," he said, "it is not power that's given me. It's a burden; it's a duty" ' (p. 13).

The upshot is a trip to America. Don and Eleanor—accompanied by her father, her aunt, and her cousin Augustus, who is in love with her—travel to the new world to see how Don can best spend the money to benefit society. The central portion of the novel is concerned with the sea voyage and American types met on shipboard. Ford deals with his Americans in almost vitriolic fashion, singling out eccentricities and fastening upon unpleasant traits; but the Dickensian streak is not strong enough to make them very interesting. They are merely repellent.

America itself is handled in a similar fashion, with a loose, rambling, impressionistic collage of detail. In sum, America too is unpleasant, and long before the climactic news that Don can do absolutely nothing with his money, since it is securely tied to Kelleg Enterprises by his father's will, the hero has sickened of his native country. His reaction to Coney Island during a ferry-boat ride is violent. 'I'll suppress the whole thing!' (p. 265). And Broadway at night, seen from his hotel window—'the jingle and cries of blazing, contagious, jostling Broadway'—fares no better. ' "It's all hopelessly material," he muttered aloud. "There's nothing that isn't blatant, vulgar, hideous" ' (p. 284).

Don is helpless before the modern world. Eleanor braves him: 'Dear boy! If you want William Morris effects and floppy gowns this isn't surely the place to come to for them' (p. 263). Her allusion is an accurate index to the purlieus of Don's mind.

Ford's culture-conscious aesthete—believer in a rural, pseudo-medieval, aristocratic world—is metaphorically bound helpless to the mast of a ferryboat plying between Manhattan and Staten Island. Ulysses hears the sirens, but their voices are not those of beautiful maidens of the sea. They are the ubiquitous cries of the machinery of an industrial world. Instead of seduction, repulsion follows, for Don, who is committed to social progress, cannot stand what he hears and sees.

Eleanor's father—an eccentric book-reviewer who at meals stands through the first course—delineates Don's problem, which is a mirror of his own.

> Don is acting precisely as I've acted all my life. He hates modern circum-
> stances. I don't say that he wants what *I* want. He doesn't. He isn't for the
> Tory Party right or wrong. But he *is* for Aestheticism right or wrong. He
> *does*, really, want the American people to go in for certain European virtues
> —for Poetry and the Higher Thought and Rational Dress. (p. 268)

But it is Eleanor's cousin Augustus who has the final word in the portrait of Don: 'He's like the tamest sort of cat. He's an incredible ass . . .' (p. 80). (The ellipsis is Ford's.)

Don Collar Kelleg, the 'incredible ass', is clearly a younger version of Ford's famous hero—he is Christopher Tietjens without brain or back-bone. Entombed in a mausoleum of novelistic conventions that appear as quaint today as the daguerreotype, he has only to be exhumed to reveal the outlines of Ford's generic hero. He is 'excellent and gentle'

(p. 50); he is the 'noblest and best man you've ever seen' (p. 51); he has 'a remarkably developed moral sense' (p. 58); he is 'unreasonably kind' (p. 58).

Ford's gauche vanity? Hardly, though the author is clearly involved with his hero. But there is more here than that. What we see is a writer whose devotion to society, to mankind, is nothing short of reckless. So much so that for years his hero simply appears to be 'an incredible ass'. And the author himself?

> He was a longish, leanish, fairish young Englishman, not unamenable, on certain sides, to classification—as for instance by being a gentleman, by being rather specifically one of the educated, one of the generally sound and generally pleasant; yet, though to that degree neither extraordinary nor abnormal, he would have failed to play straight into an observer's hands. He was young for the House of Commons, he was loose for the army. He was refined, as might have been said, for the city, and quite apart from the cut of his cloth, he was sceptical, it might have been felt, for the church. On the other hand he was credulous for diplomacy, or perhaps even for science, while he was perhaps at the same time too much in his mere senses for poetry, and yet too little in them for art. You would have got fairly near him by making out in his eyes the potential recognition of ideas; but you would have quite fallen away again on the question of the ideas themselves. The difficulty with Densher was that he looked vague without looking weak—idle without looking empty.[3]

The vagueness that James so unerringly seized upon in Ford when he modeled Densher after him is the same vagueness that can be felt surrounding Ford's early heroes. They inhabit a vacuum of ill-defined social purpose and moral goodness.

> 'He's much too kind,' Eleanor said, and Mr Greville uttered the solitary word:
> 'Precisely!'
> 'And that means', he pursued triumphantly, 'that he hasn't any kind of system in his morality.' He turned definitely upon Don. 'You can't get through life like that!' he said seriously and with an air of shaking his head ever so minutely
> 'You mean', Don said, 'that Eleanor will never know where to have me?' (p. 58)

A silly conversation about a silly man. But move fifteen years forward. Remove the pseudo-Jamesian tone; transform a hysterical Don and a stuffy Eleanor into an enraged Sylvia and a set-upon Christopher; interject real conflict into the endless dialectical analyses. For Sylvia does not at all *know where to have* Christopher.

> 'You want to know why I hate my husband. I'll tell you; it's because of his simple, sheer immorality. I don't mean his actions; his views! Every speech he utters about everything makes me—I swear it makes me—in spite of myself, want to stick a knife into him, and I can't prove he's wrong, not ever, about the simplest thing.'4

In reality, it is the humanity, the morality, of Christopher's views which bothers her. 'He'll profess that murderers ought to be preserved in order to breed from because they're bold fellows, and innocent children executed because they're sick' (p. 40). And 'he's so formal he can't do without all the conventions there are and so truthful he can't use half of them' (p. 32). 'But what does he want?' asks Perowne, with whom Sylvia has been having an affair. ' "He wants," Sylvia said, "to play the part of Jesus Christ" ' (p. 379).

There is something of the same fool about Christopher as there is about Don, and the premise underlying their conduct is one that Ford, the child of Pre-Raphaelitism, never stopped believing. Eleanor's father says at one point in the novel: 'The man's a poet: that's what the trouble is' (p. 235). And at the end of the novel, Canzano writes to her: 'My Dear, Don is a genius.' But poet-geniuses do not inhabit the world of real men—at least not without making fools of themselves. The castles of thought in which the Aesthetic Movement dwelt proved this. And yet the world of real men is the lifeline of the novel. Jettison this world and you write make-believe. You live in fairyland.

There is nothing in *An English Girl* to justify calling Don either a 'poet' or a 'genius'. His conduct is simply ludicrous. Christopher is a more baffling case, and hence far more real. With his abilities he should have been 'Lord Chancellor or Chancellor of the Exchequer' (p. 432). Sylvia says to him: 'What could you not have risen to with your gifts, and your influence . . . and your integrity.' And Macmaster, Tietjens' friend and coworker in the Office of Statistics, sees the same brilliance in him: 'He had no doubt that Tietjens was the most brilliant man in England of that day, so that nothing caused him more anguish than the thought that Tietjens might not make a brilliant and rapid career towards some illustrious position in the public services' (p. 48). Christopher disappoints each of them, but it is not for lack of talent. Ford distributes the blame more subtly.

There is one crucial difference between Don Collar Kelleg and Christopher Tietjens. Both are out of joint with society and their time, but Tietjens is sure of his ground, Don is not.

> 'What you ought to do', Mr Greville said, 'is to find yourself.'
> He hadn't got to bother about trains of thought, but about what he wanted. And Mr Greville hazarded the further speech:
> 'If a man is determined to inflict himself on his time it is his duty first to consider what *he is*! For what is criminal is to wobble once you have begun. A man has to define what his ideal is and then to make for it.'
> 'Ah,' Don said, 'that is what people have been telling me all my life. . . .'
> (p. 127)

Christopher may waver and totter dangerously as society besieges him, but he will never desert his beliefs. Don is unable to discover what he should believe. He does wobble. He deserts America, then reverses himself and deserts Eleanor for America at the end of the novel. Thus the story leaves off where it should begin. And it is for Christopher, many years later, to go on slowly and painfully to discover both his role in an alien world and ways to cope with a society devoid of meaning.

Thus when it is no longer Ford's hero who is baffled by society, but *society* that is baffled by the hero, Christopher Tietjens emerges, larger than life—a generic portrait—neither incredible nor an ass; and the qualities that before made Ford's hero ludicrous and pathetic will in *Parade's End* make him human, and perhaps even more than human.

If Ford had to sever the umbilical cord that linked him to the Aesthetic Movement to obtain maturity in his art, he also had to free himself from the Jamesian vision. This overmastering vision of the world obscured Ford's personal subjects from him for years; the Jamesian world was neither the England Ford knew, the England of Edward Ashburnham and Tietjens, nor the America he had visited in 1906, the America of Florence and Dowell and the Misses Hurlbird. Ford's token handling of the 'international theme' in *An English Girl* demonstrates how unfordian the subject matter really is, for it is only in a closing letter from Canzano to Eleanor, after the action of the novel is over, that the theme is finally asserted.

You are cowardly—all you English are cowardly: you are afraid of your own emotions: you are afraid that if you become passionate you will lose dignity. That's why you insist on maintaining your frigid exteriors. (p. 307)

Remove the Jamesian overlay here, and what remains is something very close to the matter of *The Good Soldier* and *Parade's End*. The emotions, passion, hover underneath the Jamesian veneer, which conceals and disguises even from the author what his proper subject matter is. For it is there—in the story of Eleanor and her cousin Augustus, who is in love with her.

'Oggie dear,' she said softly, 'oughtn't a man—a man of our class—to be less a slave of his passions?' (p. 180)

But Ford will not let his cardboard characters enter the real world.

'Oh, you intolerable woman!' he brought out like a curse: 'one is or one isn't. Do you suppose I *want* to love you? I'd give my eyesight and my hearing and my taste and my touch not to care for you. Do you suppose I am "indulging" in something? Why, you talk like a temperance reformer telling a sot to abstain from drink. I'm not drinking, am I? I don't get any pleasure out of it.'
'Well, Oggie dear,' she said, 'I'm not blaming you, I asked you a question. I don't know how men are made. I thought you ought to be able to find distractions.' (p. 180)

Eleanor's empty words have swallowed the latent plot. Further talk only dissipates the conflict, while the surprise appearance of Oggie's mother on the scene proves to be not a complication but an irrelevancy.

'I don't see what's to be done,' she said. She sat still, rather depressed, looking at the paste buckles on her shoes that, in the moonlight, shot direful rays at her eyes as the boat swayed a little. 'I'm sorry for you. But I can't mend anything.'
'Yes, I know you're sorry,' he said, 'you've been very decent to me.'
An odd, draped, white object poked itself from the hatchway beside them, and in the pale stillness had a ghostly semblance of pricking up fantastic ears.
Augustus's voice hissed out:
'I see you mother. Come and listen if you want to listen. But, by God, you're driving me to suicide. It's as much murder as if you put arsenic in my toast.' He was shaking violently in his dancing slippers, his face grew even bluer in tinge. And accompanied by a deep exasperation from Augustus the figure turned its face below the level of the deck. His mother had gone to find Don. (pp. 180–81)

That is all Ford can make of it. Along with Aunt Emmeline's foot-steps this particular plot strand disappears into the night, for although Augustus talks of suicide, no one, least of all the reader, takes him seriously. Nor is Don ever allowed to learn of Oggie's love. Ford, perhaps unconsciously, has avoided conflict by allowing Aunt Emmeline, instead of Don, to overhear the two.

Now consider the same subject matter, the same basic scene, eight years later in *The Good Soldier*, told this time by a narrator. Dowell is reconstructing in his mind what must have happened on the night his wife Florence overheard Edward Ashburnham, her lover, declare his love for another. Dowell himself was not present. Indeed, he wasn't even aware that his wife had been unfaithful to him until after her suicide. Thus he is only now piecing out the events of the evening on which Florence learned that Ashburnham had forsaken her for his ward, Nancy Rufford. It was immediately after this that Florence committed suicide.

'It was a very black night.' Florence was dressed all in black, because she was in mourning for a deceased cousin. 'The girl [Nancy] was dressed in cream-coloured muslin, and must have glimmered under the tall trees of the dark park like a phosphorescent fish in a cupboard. You couldn't have had a better beacon.'[5] The Casino orchestra was playing the Rakóczy march. Florence came creeping over the short grass behind the public bench on which the two sat.

> Anyhow, there you have the picture: the immensely tall trees, elms most of them, towering and feathering away up into the black mistiness that trees seem to gather about them at night; the silhouettes of those two upon the seat; the beams of light coming from the Casino, the woman all in black peeping with fear behind the tree-trunk. It is melodrama; but I can't help it. (p. 110)

Now this, we are sure, is very great art, even before we know why we think as we do. To put it simply, it has the ring of truth—and yet, if one thinks about it for a moment, this second scene is more unbelievable than its counterpart in *An English Girl*. 'It is melodrama. . . .' Why, then, does it seem so believable?

In the first place, Ford has shifted the level at which he is approaching his subject matter. In *An English Girl* Eleanor and Oggie are simply too well-behaved to act improperly. They are mannequins with Jamesian sensibilities inhabiting a world composed of empty verbal formulae. In *The Good Soldier* the same politeness rules the world of Nauheim, yet hidden underneath the surface, and exposed only gradually, are lechery, adultery, feigned illness, blackmail, suicide, and insanity. That is, the suppressed ugliness of *An English Girl* breaks through the surface. (The correspondences between the two scenes, of course, are not one-to-one. Oggie's infatuation is the archetype of Ashburnham's incurable love of Nancy; Don is in the position of Dowell, the deceived narrator; Aunt Emmeline's role is that of Florence; and Eleanor's position, in this scene at least, is comparable to Nancy's.)

The point is that the outward show of manners is no longer equated with reality. In addition, double-lives means double-plot, and the disparity between the two lives of each of the characters, between the appearance and the reality, is heightened by turning the second series of events into melodrama.

The melodrama is believable because of a shift of atttitude on the part of the author. An ironic tone has entered the story through the voice of the narrator; and because of his disbelief, his doubt that what has happened could really have happened, Dowell makes us accept the scene as a representation of the real world.

> And that miserable woman must have got it in the face, good and strong. It must have been horrible for her. Horrible! Well, I suppose she deserved all that she got. (p. 110)

Dowell's doubt of the significance of it all insures credibility. And, one might add, so does the plot-structure, the dislocated time-sequence. We know of Florence's suicide before we learn its cause. Thus our attention is held by the acts of reconstruction which the narrator performs as he gradually discovers the true meaning of the events of the past nine years.

In *An English Girl* there is no such emergence of meaning, for in Ford's hand the Jamesian dialectic does not create tension and complexity. Instead of tautness, there is gush; instead of involvement, simplification. In James, on the other hand, it spells conflict; indeed, it often becomes the center of conflict, the fire over which James's characters are set to roast on moral spits.

Just as Ford had erroneously assumed that James's world could be his, so too he made the false assumption that his method could be. He sensed, quite rightly, that James was incapable of telling a story straight. And he himself suffered from the same disease. Whatever the reason in James's case, and perhaps that will always remain a mystery, Ford's was simply that he could not bear conflict. In his personal life, he was known to become torturously involved in a situation, rendering it unbearable, because he could not face things directly and resolve them. In his early novels there is a marked absence of real conflict. It goes skittering off the page with Aunt Emmeline. Hence the appeal of the Jamesian dialectic. It rendered complexity; it created tensions: it appeared to be the source of conflict in James's novels. It was not, of course. The substance of conflict stems from the nature of man coming into collision with the conventions of society. This Ford was to learn; indeed, it became his major theme in both *The Good Soldier* and *Parade's End*. One reason Ford was eventually to develop the time-shift was to cope with his inadequacy to handle conflict; *it* became his dialectical tool, the means for probing beneath the surface of society. A second reason is perhaps not quite so obvious.

Son of a German émigré, and grandson of a Pre-Raphaelite painter, Ford was twice removed from the mainstream of English society. His problem was no easier than the deracinated Conrad's, no less critical than the expatriate James's. None of the three could write of English manners with the ease, say, of E. M. Forster. James needed point of view and centers of consciousness; Conrad, Marlow and an inversive method. Ford turned to the time-shift, and, later, the stream of consciousness, to figure and justify in his art his personal disinvolvement from the society which is its subject.

Ford most desired to be the historian. He wanted to register his own times in terms of his own time. And it is from this desire that a large part of his admiration for James stems, for the greatness of the master, 'to put it succinctly, is that of the historian—the historian of one, of two, and possibly of three or more, civilizations'. 'He, more than anybody, has faithfully rendered his observations for us.'[6] But neither James's perspective nor his rendering of society could be Ford's. And the lesson he finally learned from the master was just that. James, writing in the *Notebooks* of his plans for *The Wings of the Dove*, said: 'But one can do so little with English adultery—it is so much less inevitable, and so much more ugly in all its hiding and lying side.'[7] Ford's answer is *The Good Soldier* and *Parade's End*. Influences, Ford once remarked, 'are queer things, and there is no knowing when or where they may take you'.[8]

SOURCE: *Kenyon Review*, XXII (1960).

NOTES

1. *Henry James* (London, 1913; New York, 1915) pp. 90–91.
2. *An English Girl* (1907) p. 7.
3. Henry James, *Wings of the Dove* (New York, 1946), p. 54.
4. *Parade's End* (New York, 1950) p. 39.
5. *The Good Soldier* (New York, 1951) p. 109.
6. *Henry James*, pp. 22, 48.
7. *The Notebooks of Henry James* (New York, 1947) p. 170.
8. Preface to *Collected Poems* (1916) p. 22.

MARK SCHORER

The Good Soldier: an interpretation (1948, 1951)

LEARNING to read novels, we slowly learn to read ourselves. A few years ago, writing of Ford Madox Ford, Herbert Gorman said: 'If he enlarged upon himself he was quite justified in doing so and it seems to me that the time has come now for somebody to enlarge upon him.' I translate this remark to mean that the good novelist sees himself as the source of a subject that, when it has taken its form in his work, we may profitably examine because our analysis will bring it back to ourselves, perhaps to kiss us, more likely to slap us in the face—either way, to tell us where *we* are. These are the fruits of criticism.

The time had indeed come, and today we are hearing again about Ford Madox Ford in a way that we have not heard of him for twenty years—for until recently he has had to survive as best he could in the person of Conrad's collaborator and of that brilliant editor who said to the young D. H. Lawrence that his first novel had 'every fault that the English novel can have' and that his second was 'a rotten work of genius'. The always present friend of all the great, the abettor of all the promising young, Ford was great in his own right, and now Time indeed seems ready at last, as Herbert Gorman predicted that it would, to 'weed out his own accomplishments'.

He began work on *The Good Soldier* on his fortieth birthday—the 17th of December in 1913—and he himself thought that it was his first really serious effort in the novel. 'I had never really tried to put into any novel of mine *all* that I knew about writing. I had written rather desultorily a number of books—a great number—but they had all been in the nature of *pastiches*, of pieces of rather precious writing, or of *tours de force*.' This was to be the real thing, and it was; many years later he remarked of it that it was his 'best book technically, unless you read the Tietjens books as one novel, in which case the whole design appears. But I think the Tietjens books will probably "date" a good deal, whereas the other may—and indeed need—not.' It need not have; it did not.

As in most great works of comic irony, the mechanical structure of *The Good Soldier* is controlled to a degree nothing less than taut, while the structure of meaning is almost blandly open, capable of limitless refractions. One may go further, perhaps, and say that the novel renews a major lesson of all classic art: from the very delimitation of form arises the exfoliation of theme. This, at any rate, is the fact about *The Good Soldier* that gives point to John Rodker's quip that 'it is the finest French novel in the English language', which is to say that it has perfect clarity of surface and nearly mathematical poise, and—as an admirer would wish to extend the remark—a substance at once exact and richly enigmatic. As a novel, *The Good Soldier* is like a hall of mirrors, so constructed that, while one is always looking straight ahead at a perfectly solid surface, one is made to contemplate not the bright surface itself, but the bewildering maze of past circumstances and future consequence that—somewhat falsely—it contains. Or it is like some structure all of glass and brilliantly illuminated, from which one looks out upon a sable jungle and ragged darkness.

The Good Soldier carries the subtitle 'A Tale of Passion', and the book's controlling irony lies in the fact that passionate situations are related by a narrator who is himself incapable of passion, sexual and moral alike. His is the true *accidia*, and so, from his opening absurdity: 'This is the saddest story I have ever heard', on to the end and at every point, we are forced to ask: 'How can we believe *him*? His must be exactly the *wrong* view.' The fracture between the character of the event as we feel it to be and the character of the narrator as he reports the event to us is the essential irony, yet it is not in any way a simple one; for the narrator's view as we soon discover, is not so much the wrong view as merely *a* view, although a special one. No simple inversion of statement can yield up the truth, for the truth is the maze, and, as we learn from what is perhaps the major theme of the book, appearances have their reality.

First of all, this novel is about the difference between convention and fact. The story consists of the narrator's attempt to adjust his reason to the shattering discovery that, in his most intimate relationships, he has, for nine years, mistaken the conventions of social behavior for the actual human fact. That he did not want it otherwise, that the deception was in effect self-induced, that he could not have lived at all with the actuality, is, for the moment, beside our point, although ultimately, for the attitude and the architecture of the novel, it is the whole point.

The narrator and his wife, Florence, are wealthy Americans; the friends with whom they are intimately concerned, Edward and Leonora Ashburnham, are wealthy English people. Together, these four seem to be the very bloom of international society; they are all, as the narrator repeatedly tells us, 'good people', and the Ashburnhams are even that special kind of good people, 'good county people'. Florence is a little pathetic, because she suffers from heart trouble and must be protected against every shock and exposure. Leonora is perhaps a little strong-willed in the management of her domestic affairs, but these have been very trying and in their cause she has been altogether splendid and self-sacrificing, a noblewoman. Edward is nearly flawless: 'the fine soldier, the excellent landlord, the extraordinarily kind, careful, and in-dustrious magistrate, the upright, honest, fair-dealing, fair-thinking, public character ... the model of humanity, the hero, the athlete, the father of his country, the law-giver'. For nine years these four have enjoyed an apparently placid and civilized friendship, visiting back and forth, meeting annually at Nauheim, where they take the seasonal hypochondriac baths, sharing in one another's interests and affairs. Then comes the tremendous, the stunning reversal: when illness proves to be a lusterless debauchery; domestic competence the maniacal will of the tigress, the egoistic composure of the serpent; heroic masculinity the most sentimental libertinism. And the narrator, charged at the end with the responsibility of caring for a little mad girl, Edward's last love, is left to relate his new knowledge of an exposed reality to his long untroubled faith in its appearance. Which he is not able to do, of course; as which of us could?

But are not these 'realities', in effect, 'appearances'? Are not the 'facts' that the narrator discovers in themselves 'conventions' of a sort? We are forced, at every point, to look back at this narrator, to scan his beguiling surprise, to measure the angle of refraction at which that veiled glance penetrates experience. He himself suggests that we are looking at events here as one looks at the image of a mirror in a mirror, at the box within the box, the arch beyond the arch beyond the arch. All on one page we find these reversals: 'Upon my word, yes, our intimacy was like a minuet. ... No, by God, it is false! It wasn't a minuet that we stepped; it was a prison—a prison full of screaming hysterics. . . . And yet I swear by the sacred name of my creator that it was true. It was true sunshine; the true music; the true plash of the fountains from the mouths of stone dolphins. For, if for me we were four people with the same tastes, with the same desires, acting—or, no, not acting—sitting here and there unanimously, isn't that the truth?' The appearance had its reality. How, then, does the 'reality' suggest that it is something less—or more?

Why is Florence always 'poor Florence' or 'that poor wretch' or 'that poor cuckoo'? Why the persistent denigration of tone? Why can Florence not be charged with something less trivial and vulgar than 'making eyes at Edward'? The narrator has something to gain in Florence's loss, and that is a fragment of self-esteem. If Florence is a harlot, she is so, in part, because of her husband's fantastic failure, but if we can be persuaded of her calculated vice and of her nearly monstrous malice, her husband appears before us as the pathetic victim of life's ironic circumstance. What, again, is the meaning of the narrator's nearly phobic concern with Catholicism, or of the way in which his slurs at Leonora are justified by her attachment to that persuasion? This is a mind not quite in balance. And again, Leonora's loss is Edward's gain, and Edward's gain at last is the narrator's gain. For why are Florence's indiscretions crimes, and Edward's, with Florence, follies at worst, and at best true goodnesses of heart? Why, after his degradation, is Edward still 'a fine fellow'? In every case, the 'fact' is somewhere between the mere social convention and that different order of convention which the distorted understanding of the narrator imposes upon them.

Yet the good novelist does not let us rest here. These distortions are further revelations. Mirror illuminates mirror, each arch marks farther distances. Ford tells us that he suggested the title, *The Good Soldier*, 'in hasty irony', when the publisher's objections to *The Saddest Story* became imperative; and while, under the circumstances of 1915, the new title must have seemed, for this novel and for this real soldier, Ford, peculiarly inappropriate, certainly uncongenial enough to cause the author understandable 'horror', it is nevertheless very useful to readers today, so accustomed to war that the word 'soldier' no longer carries its special force. The novel designates Edward as the good soldier, as Edward has seen Imperial service in India. For Edward the narrator has the strongest affection and his only forgiveness. Of him, he says: 'I guess that I myself, in my fainter way, come into the category of the passionate, of the headstrong, and the too-truthful. [This is his weirdest absurdity, the final, total blindness of infatuation, and self-infatuation.] For I can't conceal from myself the fact that I loved Edward Ashburnham—and that I love him because he was just myself. If I had had the courage and the virility and possibly also the physique of Edward Ashburnham I should, I fancy, have done much what he did. He seems to me like a large elder brother who took me out on several excursions and did many dashing things whilst I just watched him robbing the orchards, from a distance. And, you see, I am just as much of a sentimentalist as he was. . . .' Niggardly, niggardly half-truth!—for observe the impossible exceptions: courage, virility, physique! What sane man could expect them? The narrator aspires to be 'the good soldier', the conventionally fine fellow, yet has no expectation of ever being in the least like him in any but his most passive features, and these working not at the level of sexuality, as with Edward, but of malformed friendship. To understand the exact significance here, we must turn, perhaps, to another book.

In his dedicatory epistle in the 1927 edition Ford says that he hoped *The Good Soldier* would do in English something of the sort that Maupassant's *Fort comme la Mort* did in French. The remark is suggestive in the structural terms that Ford must have had in mind; I wish, however, to call attention to what may be the most accidental connection of theme. Of one of his characters Maupassant says: 'He was an old intellectual who might have been, perhaps, a good soldier, and who could never console himself for what he had not been.'

The vicious consolations of failure form our narrator. 'Men,' said D. H. Lawrence, 'men can suck the heady juice of exalted self-importance from the bitter weed of failure—failures are usually the most conceited of men.' Thus at the end of the novel we have forgotten the named good soldier, and we look instead at the nominated one, the narrator himself. His consolations are small: attendance upon the ill, 'seeing them through'—for twelve years his wife, for the rest of his life the mad girl whom he fancies he might have loved; yet they give him a function, at least. This is the bitter, paltry destiny that, he thinks, life has forced upon him; thus he need never see himself as bitter or as paltry—or, indeed, as even telling a story.

And thus we come to the final circles of meaning, and these, like ripples round a stone tossed into a pool, never stop. For, finally, *The Good Soldier* describes a world that is without moral point, a narrator who suffers from the madness of moral inertia. 'You ask how it feels to be a deceived husband. Just heavens, I do not know. It feels just nothing at all. It is not hell, certainly it is not necessarily heaven. So I suppose it is the intermediate stage. What do they call it? Limbo.' *Accidia!* It is the dull hysteria of sloth that besets him, the sluggish insanity of defective love. 'And, yes, from that day forward she always treated me and not Florence as if I were the invalid.' 'Why, even to me she had the air of being submissive—to me that not the youngest child will ever pay heed to. Yes, this is the saddest story. . . .' The saddest story? One may say this another way, and say the same thing. *The Good Soldier* is a comedy of humor, and the humor is phlegm.

It is in the comedy that Ford displays his great art. Irony, which makes no absolute commitments and can thus enjoy the advantage of many ambiguities of meaning and endless complexities of situation, is at the same time an evaluative mood, and, in a master, a sharp one. Perhaps the most astonishing achievement in this astonishing novel is the manner in which the author, while speaking through his simple, infatuated character, lets us know how to take his simplicity and his infatuation. This is comic genius. It shows, for example, in the character- istic figures, the rather simple-minded and, at the same time, grotesquely comic metaphors: a girl in a white dress in the dark is 'like a phosphor- escent fish in a cupboard'; Leonora glances at the narrator, and he feels 'as if for a moment a lighthouse had looked at me'; Leonora, boxing the ears of one of Edward's little mistresses, 'was just striking the face of an intolerable universe'. Figures such as these, and they occur in abundance, are the main ingredient in Ford's tone, and they are the subtle supports of such broader statements as this: 'I should marry Nancy if her reason were ever sufficiently restored to let her appreciate the meaning of the Anglican marriage service. But it is probable that her reason will never be sufficiently restored to let her appreciate the meaning of the Anglican marriage service. Therefore I cannot marry her, according to the law of the land.' This is a mode of comic revela- tion and evaluation less difficult, perhaps, than that which is evident in Ford's figures of speech, but to sustain it as he does, with never a rupture of intent, is the highest art.

Then there are the wonderfully comic events—little Mrs Maidan dead in a trunk with her feet sticking out, as though a crocodile had caught her in its giant jaws, or the poor little mad girl saying to the narrator after weeks of silence: 'Shuttlecocks!' There are the frequent moments when the author leads his characters to the most absurd anticlimaxes (as when, at the end of the fourth chapter, Leonora, in a frenzy of self-important drama, demands: 'Don't you know that I'm an Irish Catholic?'), and then, with superb composure, Ford leads his *work* away from the pit of bathos into which his people have fallen. There is the incessant wit, of style and statement, the wittier for its deceptive clothing of pathos. And, most important in this catologue of comic devices, there is the covering symbolism of illness: characters who fancy that they suffer from 'hearts', who do suffer defective hearts not, as they would have us believe, in the physiological but in the moral sense, and who are told about by a character who has no heart at all, and hence no mind. 'I never', he tells us with his habitually comic solemnity, 'I never was a patient anywhere.' To which we may add: only always, in the madhouse of the world.

Is *The Good Soldier*, perhaps, a novelist's novel? Ford thought that it was his best work, and his judgment was always the judgment of the craftsman. Certainly it can tell us more about the nature of the novel than most novels or books about them: the material under perfect control, the control resulting in the maximum meaning, the style precisely evaluating that meaning. But if it is a kind of archetype of the processes of fiction, if, that is to say, it can demonstrate his craft to the craftsman, then it can also help all of us to read. And is it not true that, once we learn how to read, even if then we do not live more wisely, we can at least begin to be aware of why we have not? *The Good Soldier*, like all great works, has the gift and power of remorse.

SOURCE: M. Schorer, *The World We Imagine* (1948, 1968).

JOHN A. MEIXNER

The Saddest Story (1960)

'I HAVE always been mad about writing'—it is Ford Madox Ford, of course—and from an early time 'made enthusiastic studies into how words should be handled and novels constructed'. Yet, paradoxically, Ford himself, as he has told us, did not attempt to put into his own novels '*all*' that he knew about writing until he was forty. That appropriate time did arrive, however; and late in 1913 he set to work 'to show what I could do'—'and,' he added, 'the *Good Soldier* resulted.' Of the book's high value, Ford, as various comments indicate, was fully assured. Two years before his death, he even went so far as to call it his only novel 'at all to count'.[1]

Most readers will readily debate whether *Some Do Not* at least does not also 'count'. But there can be no question that in his estimate of the worth of *The Good Soldier* Ford was thoroughly justified. For the book is, in fact, one of the literary triumphs of the twentieth century—a work of the very highest art which must also be ranked among the more powerful novels that have been written. Certainly very few works in English—*The Scarlet Letter, Jude the Obscure, Sons and Lovers, The House in Paris* perhaps—can match the force of its emotion, while none can equal its duration. And this emotional intensity, which begins on a high pitch in the opening chapter, not only sustains itself throughout but, in fact, steadily tightens until the final moments. The psychological effect of the novel is that of some relentless spiral cutting deeper and deeper into its human material. It is the extraordinary 'turning of the screw', not for 140 pages as in James's famous nouvelle, but for a far more exacting 256, and rendered with a visceral intensity completely unknown to James—one we are more likely to associate with the Greeks. *The Good Soldier*, in short, is a rare combination of Flaubertian technique and almost Dostoevskian laceration and power. It is also a book, it is extremely important to add, whose second reading is startlingly different from its first, in intellectual subtlety, in tone, and, above all, in feeling.

Originally calling his novel 'The Saddest Story'—its title when its opening chapters appeared in the famous first number of *Blast* (June 20, 1914)—Ford was compelled to change this name because of the war. For, as his publisher, John Lane, insisted, such a title as 'The Saddest Story' to a book brought out in 1915, the darkest days of battle, would only doom it. Appealed to for a substitute, Ford, by this time in the army, suggested with irony to Lane 'The Good Soldier'—and was, he says, horrified when six months later the novel appeared under that title, with the sentence, 'This is the saddest story I have ever heard', inserted at the beginning, as a kind of saving remnant. This change Ford never ceased to regret, and only fear of confusion prevented him from restoring the original after the war. Indeed, that events compelled him to alter his title was, it should be stressed, among the more unfortunate incidents in his often unfortunate career. For as guide to Ford's intention, 'The Saddest Story' is far more appropriate than its present one—the most obvious, if not really the most important, defect of which is its misleading indication that the book is about war. It must be granted, of course, that 'The Good Soldier' as descriptive of its central character, Edward Ashburnham (and perhaps also of its narrator) is essentially on the mark. But the meaning and significance of the book spring not from the story of only one individual but from the inter-relationship of all its characters and events, from its total pattern. Had the novel become known as 'The Saddest Story', the title would, in its superlative, even vaunting claim (even in its touch of banality), almost surely have challenged both critics and general readers to meet the book on the very highest terms, a confrontation which even yet has not been made.

Robie Macauley, for example, writing in *The Kenyon Review*, for all his high praise and perceptive comments, classifies the novel as a 'miniature' performance and suggests that, were it not for the fact of the Tietjens books, it might be thought of as 'the lucky try of a gifted and fortunate minor novelist'. Misreading the relationship between Ashburnham and his wife, Mr Macauley formulates a partial, even mistaken meaning for the novel, and so misses the great scope of the work asserted by its original title. It is not surprising, therefore, that he should dismiss that title by saying that Ford 'was always bad at naming his books'.[2]

Mr Macauley, however, is far closer to the spirit of the novel than Mark Schorer, whose critique strategically appears at the head of the 1951 and 1957 reissues of the book. Unlike Mr Macauley, Mr Schorer sympathizes with Ford's 'understandable' horror at the change. Yet his argument is not that the original was more truly expressive, but that the present title, apparently because of the 'libertine' character of Edward Ashburnham, is 'peculiarly inappropriate, certainly uncongenial enough'. Unfortunately, these same words are far more applicable to Mr Schorer's analysis. For despite his high estimation of *The Good Soldier* (he in fact deems it a great work), the book in his hands loses much of its real importance and becomes little more than a clever *tour de force*. By focusing on only one dimension, Mr Schorer has unhappily described and treated a novel of deep, intensely tragic power as a comedy and, more unhappily still, as a 'comedy of humor'.

The culminating achievement of Ford's 'cat's cradle' vision, *The Good Soldier* is, at its core, a tragedy. It tells a lacerating tale of groping human beings, caught implacably by training, character, and circumstance, who cruelly and blindly inflict on each other terrible misery and pain: 'poor wretches', as the narrator says, 'creeping over this earth in the shadow of an eternal wrath'. Yet around this awful core, and without diminishing its power, Ford in his complex and subtle art has placed a context of comic irony. This context—which Mr Schorer has made the center of the book—Ford uses, as we shall see, to provide the novel's ultimate commentary on the nature of human life in the twentieth century world. Indeed, in its juxtaposition of these two modes, *The Good Soldier* epitomizes in a classic way the altered tragic vision of our modern sensibility.

Let us examine its action more closely. At the heart of *The Good Soldier* is a tormented love triangle bridging two generations. Ford tells us that in writing the work he sought 'to do for the English novel what in *Forte comme la Mort* Maupassant has done for the French'. And the triangle he establishes is essentially Maupassant's in that book. An older man, hopelessly in love with a younger woman, agonizingly stumbles to his doom—caught in a passion as strong as death. In Ford's hands, however, the basic triangle has undergone a fascinating, original transplantation. The older pair become husband and wife, not lover and mistress, and the girl is herself swept away by the action. The cultural situation is thoroughly anglicized, and the drama made enormously more taut, integrated, and powerful. A further change is the adding of two other characters, a wealthy, somewhat bizarre American couple, Florence and John Dowell. For many pages, in fact, the reader is led to believe that the novel is about a four-sided relationship among the Dowells and the Ashburnhams—or, more precisely, about a different triangle, for the American wife, it is soon disclosed, has been Ashburnham's mistress. Only gradually, as the novel moves through a series of bewildering turns in which the 'truth' of what unfolds continually shifts—seeming actualities exposed as substanceless or as profound distortions—does the reader finally confront the central trio.

In essence, then, this is the action of *The Good Soldier*; but to understand its issues we must go still deeper into its chief characters and events. It will also significantly help clarity to straighten out the intricately rearranged chronology of the book and to review the steps, down almost a score of years, which developed the intense marital hostility between the Ashburnhams.

The nature of their conflict was simple, inevitable, and irreconcilable. In the parentally arranged marriage of the young couple were yoked two critically inharmonious personalities, in temperament, rearing, religion, and conception of the good life. In his actions, Edward—'the good soldier'—was guided by idealistic and sentimental values. Raised in the generous, responsible traditions of his family long established on their English land, he was noted for his paternal acts of kindness to hard-pressed tenants and hapless townspeople and for a selfless bravery. Practical, even materialistic values, on the other hand, motivated the ungenerous Leonora, the product of a beleagured, impoverished English father supporting a large family of girls in a hostile and exploited Ireland. In contrast to her easy-going Anglican husband, Leonora was a strict, convent-educated Roman Catholic.

At first hidden, these differences eventually grew prominent. To Leonora, Edward's generosities were a wild extravagance leading to swift ruin. She suffered also from his insistence that their sons must be raised traditionally as Anglicans; and her barrenness she took as a judgment of God. Under these anguished pressures, the latent coldness and efficiency of Leonora's personality grew ascendant—a development which could only alienate a man like Edward. For with his sentimental, pre-twentieth century view of the cosmos, he expected women to be fragile, flowerlike creatures, sympathetic, tender, and providers of moral support for their men. What held the Ashburnhams together was, above all, their marriage vows: as a Roman Catholic, Leonora was unable to divorce, and Edward, as a gentleman, would not. Besides this, Leonora felt a strong physical passion for her handsome husband—an attraction which, to her anguish, he never felt for her. And Edward, on his part, profoundly respected and admired, even feared, his wife for her strength of character and purposefulness. (The text does not warrant Robie Macauley's interpretation that the other women in Edward's life were merely substitutes for his true love, Leonora—that the Ashburnhams 'can love each other only through a third person'. Edward's positive feeling for his wife is never deeper than respect; all else about her repels his spirit. Mr Macauley's assertion that Ford by his original title meant to say 'that the saddest story is the perpetual story of love between man and woman, love that can never quite arrive at understanding and decays' is, as far as it goes, valid enough. But this theme does not require any notion of a third person intermediary between the Ashburnhams. Unjustified also is his statement that Leonora's character is 'as equally right and wrong, equally good and evil' as Edward's. For a while, no doubt, that is part of Ford's dramatic illusion; it is not what he is saying.)

But, in time, Edward's dissatisfaction and events led him to look outward for the feminine warmth his nature required, so that the history of the Ashburnhams involved not one or two, but actually a succession of triangles, both in England and the East. Through them all Leonora, sustained by the managerial labors she had wrested to herself, anguishedly but discreetly kept silent, in the blind belief that Edward, having tried the various womanly types, would come at last to hers. As she saw it, her duty as a Catholic Englishwoman was to hold her husband and to prevent scandal. Not even the annexation of Edward by Florence Dowell, the American wife, which began at Nauheim on their return from India and which was to last for nine years, could shake this increasingly bitter faith. At last, however, Edward came to his ultimate passion, his young ward Nancy Rufford—a love which ended one taut situation for the Ashburnhams, in that Florence despairingly took her life, but began another that was to be far more terrible.

A queer, angelic, extremely sensitive girl of twenty-two, Nancy Rufford seemed almost a daughter to Leonora and Edward. To her thoroughly innocent, convent-trained eyes, the Ashburnhams were perfectly married; Edward in particular she had always adored, seeing him as a cross between Lohengrin and the Chevalier Bayard. And he, on discovering his fierce, powerful desire for this beloved almost-daughter, as fiercely determined to leave her alone.

The ensuing months were a time of intensest agony for all three—and are the emotional core of the book. For Edward, in the torment of his self-denial and the knowledge that life could offer him no spiritual completion: constant drinking and a steady, slow dying. For Leonora, understanding his passion, and his decision (and hating and admiring him for it): anguish, dull headaches, and a bitter stoical round of duties. And for the girl: the gradual discovery of the true situation and of Edward's love for her—a knowledge which she clasped triumphantly to her heart, perceiving the depth of her responding love for him. Deciding at last to send Nancy to her father in India, Edward clung, however, to the sentimental hope that she would continue to love him —a wish he revealed to his enraged wife, with terrible consequences. For Leonora, determining to crush such a hope, vindictively exposed to the girl the full story of her husband's infidelities and of her suffering and humiliation. And in endless talks in the night, Leonora would also hammer at the girl that she must marry him and save his life—while simultaneously impressing upon her that in the eyes of their Church it could never be a marriage and would mean the girl's eternal damnation. The complex attractions and repulsions among the three characters are electrifying, the most terrible moment occuring when Nancy, in all her naive cruelty, appeared at Edward's bed and offered herself to him: 'I can never love you now I know the kind of man you are. I will belong to you to save your life. But I can never love you.' (In anguish, Edward ordered her from his room.) With the departure of the girl, affairs at Branshaw settled to a calmer tenor—until a telegram from Nancy (sent from Brindisi) arrived for Ashburnham. So atrociously heartless is the message that Edward, for whom the girl and the love between them is the only meaning in life, kills himself by cutting his throat—horribly, with a penknife. A little later, when the eastward-sailing Nancy reads of his suicide in an Aden newspaper, she becomes permanently mad. Eventually, Dowell, who also had been in love with the girl, brings her back to the Ashburnham house which he has pur-chased, cast once again in the role of nursemaid. Meanwhile, Leonora, the colder, more efficient personality, has remarried, this time to a more ordinary human type; and, as the book ends, she is expecting a child who will be raised a Romanist. Leonora at last will have her 'quiet, comfortable, good time'.

Rudyard Kipling once wrote that 'There are five-and-forty ways to indite tribal lays/ and every single one of them is right.' Ford, who often quoted this jingle, granted that stories may be told by a multitude of means. But for each story, he insisted, there is one best method. And certainly this claim is true of *The Good Soldier*, for Ford could have transmitted his lacerating tale of passion in no more effective way than through the eyes of Florence's deceived husband, John Dowell.

The artistic advantages of having Dowell narrate the story are enormous. Some are obvious and shared with almost all novels told by a first-person narrator. Characteristically the point of view heightens reality: the narrator personally witnessed and participated in these events—they must be so. The angle of vision is also an invaluable narrative convenience. A review of the action reminds us that the novel concerns itself with a steady, gradual alteration in character and relationship over a span of many years. It is the story of a long psychological struggle in which the individual incidents which crystallize a response and move a character another notch towards alienation and hatred or towards love and passion are in themselves not sharply dramatic, are like the life that most of us live from day to day. As the narrator once observes, in a key passage, the work is called 'The Saddest Story' and not 'The Ashburnham Tragedy'

> just because there was no current to draw things along to a swift and inevitable end. . . . Here were two noble people—for I am convinced that both Edward and Leonora had noble natures—here then, were two noble natures, drifting down life, like fireships afloat on a lagoon and causing miseries, heartaches, agony of the mind, and death.

To present this tale, a narrator is clearly necessary, enabling Ford to set side by side discontinuous incidents which have powerfully affected motivation. Even Dowell's name indicates his function in the story as a necessary center of composition—a 'dowell' being, as the second definition in *Webster's Unabridged Dictionary* informs us, 'a piece of wood driven into a wall, so that other pieces may be nailed to it'. (Nor is such a meaning accidental, as can be seen by examining the names of the other characters, which also subtly imply special meanings. It surely is not chance that the two tender, sympathetic women of the novel, Mrs Basil and Mrs Maisie Maidan, have been given the names of the basil herb, commonly called 'sweet basil', and of that feminine state which has been traditionally thought of as fresh, innocent, and gentle. Nor that the cold sensualist, Florence, bears the family name of 'Hurlbird' with its emotional suggestion of ideality violated—the symbolic bird so violently used. Nor that Nancy, the character whom Ford ultimately feels and presents most intensely, bears the name of Rufford, significantly combining both the double "f" of Hueffer and Ford's first name. Nor, finally, that the tormented Edward has been given the name of Ashburnham.)

Dowell as narrator holds together, however, more than a chronologically diffuse action. He also enables Ford to shape the highly complex emotional and intellectual responses he wishes to arouse in his reader. Dowell is not after all a mere narrator, a clinical witness of the story he tells. He himself is engaged in its action.

Before examining Dowell's artistic function, however, we first must try to understand his character. For certainly, superficially considered, it is baffling. Although Ford provides various facts about him—his Philadelphia origin and wealth, for example—these are minimal and tell us little about his motivation. Where Edward, Leonora, and Nancy are 'justified' with great detail and care, Dowell's background is scarcely explained at all. We learn nothing, for example, of his immediate family, nor are we given any cause, psychological or otherwise, for his lack of masculine vitality. He has no occupation: 'I suppose I ought to have done something but I didn't see any call to do it. Why does one do things?' What he originally saw in Florence is unclear. 'I just drifted in and wanted Florence', is the way he puts it: 'And, from that moment, I determined with all the obstinacy of a possibly weak nature, if not to make her mine, at least to marry her.' That he should never in twelve years of marriage have suspected either her unfaithfulness or her fraudulent invention of a bad heart, which had kept him from any conjugal claims, seems almost fantastic. In Dowell something of the common state of humanity is missing, a lack reflected in the responses of other characters. Edward, he tells us twice, thought of him as not so much a man as a woman or a solicitor. In behavior, he is often peevish, even fatuous. Ford's characterization of Dowell undeniably seems shaped under the comic spirit.

But that is only part of the story. For our sense of the objectively ludicrous in Dowell is very much qualified by the fact that we perceive his emotional life from within. He himself tells the story. And it is also qualified by our knowledge, which gradually becomes firmer and firmer, that this emotional life is that of an individual who is a psychic cripple.

In Dowell, Ford has created one of the most remarkable, certainly one of the most subtle, characterizations in modern literature. Almost completely from within he has caught and rendered the sensibility of a severely neurotic personality. Dowell is Prufrock before Prufrock, and not a mere sketch as in Eliot but a full-scale portrait. He is a man who, incapable of acting, is almost entirely feeling—a creature of pure pathos. Lonely and unrooted, Dowell is an alienated being, as he himself with fascinating indirection indicates in the opening chapters. With 'no attachments, no accumulations', 'a wanderer on the face of public resorts', always 'too polished up', he felt 'a sense almost of nakedness—the nakedness that one feels on the sea-shore or in any great open space'. That was why the Ashburnhams had meant so much to him. They had, he implies, filled a frightening void. Dowell's absurdity does not induce laughter, but rather a grave sadness. (This deeper, more human and sympathetic side of Dowell, Mr Schorer ignores; in his reading, Ford's narrator is merely a mindless, self-deluded fool, worthy of a passionate scorn.)

The narrator's spiritual invalidism is manifest in many ways—his atypical behavior, his almost painful self-deprecation, his peculiar images, and on occasion, certain incongruously repetitive and overly precise observations which Ford superbly uses to reassert this knowledge. (For example, his reference to the marriage rites of the Anglican Church and the use of the word 'trotted' in the penultimate sentence of the book.) The plainest reference to his psychological state is brought out when he describes Leonora's reaction at their initial meeting. For at first, she was cautious and probing; but then into her eyes came a warm tenderness and friendly recognition. 'It implied trust; it implied the want of any necessity for barriers.'

> By God, she looked at me as if I were an invalid—as any kind woman may look at a poor chap in a bath chair. And, yes, from that day forward she always treated me and not Florence as if I were the invalid.

'I suppose, therefore,' he continues wryly, 'that her eyes had made a favourable answer. Or, perhaps, it wasn't a favourable answer.' The same motif of himself as the patient is reinforced a few pages later.

The clinical origin of Dowell's damaged spirit is not given, but its source does not really matter. Ford has rendered the inner life of that spirit, and that is sufficient. In fact, had more been presented of Dowell's background, the emphasis would have been taken away, as it should not be, from the central characters. 'I don't know that analysis of my own psychology matters at all to this story,' Ford pointedly has his narrator write at the opening of Part Three. 'I should say that it didn't or, at any rate, that I had given enough of it.'

The appropriateness of Dowell as the medium through which the careers of the Ashburnhams and their ward is told should by now be clear. Either in actual life—as students of mental disorders well know—or in *The Good Soldier*, the neurotic sensibility, turned in on itself, is apt to be heightened above the normal in its perception of emotional pain. His consciousness will be peculiarly receptive to the ache in the universe.

Dowell's sensitivity is further intensified by the recent shock of his sudden, appalled insight into the characters of his friends and their relationships. In quick succession he had been exposed to Edward's confidences, his calmly terrible self-destruction; and the discovery that his wife had been Edward's mistress. As he begins his account, his spirit is still under the reeling impact of his new knowledge.

Dowell's anguish is also rooted in his admiration and highly personal feeling for the Ashburnhams and their ward. In particular his emotion is grounded in his deep love for Edward and Nancy, a love which finds much of its source in their embodiment of what he values in life and in the pathetic identification he makes between himself and them. The depth of his love for the girl, with her rectitude and strange, half-tortured beauty, can be discerned in almost every description and response. They are further united in that each are innocents who for the first time have confronted the full evil of the world. Indeed in the last third of the book the reader all but ceases to see events through Dowell's eyes; although they are told by him, Nancy's seems the sensibility through which they pass.

As for his feeling for Edward, it naturally is more complicated. Dowell, like Nancy, admires Ashburnham for his collective responsibility and for his virtues as a good soldier, a considerate landlord, an upright magistrate. At first, being an American, he had taken these qualities for granted. 'I guess I thought it was part of the character of any English gentleman', the duty of his rank and station. 'Perhaps that was all that it was—but I pray God to make me discharge mine as well.' If Edward had cuckolded him, Dowell could not hate him for it, for Florence did not mean that much to him really, as he comes to see, and Edward, the 'luckless devil', had suffered too much torment. Dowell's love, finally, is based on the fact that Edward was what he himself longed to be and could not be. 'I can't conceal from myself the fact that I loved Edward Ashburnham—and that I loved him because he was just myself. . . . He seems to me like a large elder brother who took me out on several excursions and did many dashing things whilst I just watched him robbing the orchards, from a distance. And, you see, I am just as much of a sentimentalist as he was . . .'

Certainly, however, it is not sufficient for the narrator of such a passionate tale merely to be sensitive to the ache of its events. Otherwise, the effect would only seem distraught and excessive. To be communicated, the emotions must be contained within order. And this risk of sentimentality, particularly dangerous in a work as emotionally ambitious as *The Good Soldier*, Ford has masterfully guarded against.

The most obvious technical resource for the control of emotion is the prevailing tone. The irony which Dowell feels is partly the product of his natural resentment against Florence, Leonora, and Edward, all of whom in varying degrees have misused him. And it is partly a personal defense, the summoning of the intellectual principle of irony to ward off painful feelings. 'Forgive my writing of these monstrous things in this frivolous manner,' he writes in one connection. 'If I did not I should break down and cry.' The irony thus provides for the novel a counterweight, a check on unbridled responses. Sensing this control, the reader can accept the passion as valid.

The greatest ironic resentment which Dowell feels is naturally directed towards Florence and Leonora. Of Florence spying on Edward and Nancy in the park by the Casino, he writes, 'And that miserable woman must have got it in the face, good and strong. It must have been horrible for her. Horrible! Well, I suppose she deserved all that she got.' Or, at another point, he comments on Florence's justification (given to Leonora) that she had deceived him because of a passion for Jimmy that was overmastering: 'Well, I always say that an overmastering passion is a good excuse for feelings. You cannot help them. And it is a good excuse for straight actions—she might have bolted with the fellow, before or after she married me. And, if they had not enough money to get along with, they might have cut their throats, or sponged on her family. . . . No, I do not think that there is much excuse for Florence.'

As for Leonora, his dislike, based on her unfeminine hardness, her selfish individualism, and her materialism, is tempered through most of the book by admiration and by his sympathy for her tortured position and deep, unsatisfied longings. Words written by Ford about James apply as well to *The Good Soldier*: 'The normal novelist presents you with the oppressor and the oppressed. Mr James presents you with the proposition, not so much that there are no such things as oppressors and oppressed, but that, even in the act of oppressing, the oppressor isn't having a very much better time than his victim.'[3] Dowell also carefully points out that Leonora's character deteriorated under the pressure of events. Florence, an unstoppable talker, broke down Leonora's pride and reserve. 'Pride and reserve', Dowell says, 'are not the only things in life; perhaps they are not even the best things. But if they happen to be your particular virtues you will go all to pieces if you let them go. And Leonora let them go.' In the end, however, when she is released by Edward's death and remarries, Dowell's dislike emerges plainly and brings at last to clear focus all the selfishness and craving for comfortable respectability at the basis of Leonora's personality. He even literally names her 'the villain of the piece'. Part of his response is personal. Several times she has sacrificed his happiness for her own, constricted, ends. But his antipathy is also based on her destruction of the two persons he most loved—the 'Beati Immaculati' (the 'Blessed Immaculates') in the words affixed to the title page—and is expressed in the bitter irony of the following: 'So Edward and Nancy found themselves steam-rolled out and Leonora survives, . . . married to a man who is rather like a rabbit. For Rodney Bayham is rather like a rabbit and I hear that Leonora is expected to have a baby in three months' time.' The most terrible ironic thrust, however, is the *coup de canon* which ends the book. With the knowledge that Edward is going to kill himself, Dowell brings Nancy's telegram to Leonora. 'She', the closing sentence reads, 'was quite pleased with it.'

Dowell's ironic view of Edward, as might be expected, is more prominent in the earlier stages of the novel, when he is still suffering from the knowledge of betrayal. Thus, his opening physical description of Edward: 'When you looked at [his eyes] carefully you saw that they were perfectly honest, perfectly straightforward, perfectly, perfectly stupid.' Or again of Edward after the Spanish dancer barred her door to him: 'I dare say that nine-tenths of what he took to be his passion for La Dolciquita was really discomfort at the thought that he had been unfaithful to Leonora. He felt uncommonly bad, that is to say—oh, unbearably bad, and he took it all to be love. Poor devil, he was incredibly naive.' Later, as Edward steadily increases in stature, Dowell's ironic tone towards him disappears, only to emerge at key moments to serve as a subtle check to excess, and as relief. Thus after Nancy has been sent away and Leonora quietly exhibits her sense of triumph, Edward is heard to say beneath his breath, '*Thou hast conquered, O pale Galilean,*' and Dowell comments: 'It was like his sentimentality to quote Swinburne.' Even Nancy, whom he presents with such tenderness, is not completely free from Dowell's irony, a check which only redoubles the sense of bitterness. Thus in describing the form of her insanity, he writes: 'She hadn't made any fuss, her eyes were quite dry and glassy. Even when she was mad Nancy could behave herself.'

Ford further guards against the dangers of a merely aching consciousness as his transmitting medium by adopting the methods of poetry. Imagery, allusion, juxtaposition, cadence—these characteristically poetic means—are all drawn upon by Dowell to formulate emotion. A man as feeling as he, if he is to be expressive, must be in fact a poet or nothing.

It is by images that Dowell seeks to communicate his feeling of a personality or a situation. Thus, he writes of Florence:

She became for me a rare and fragile object, something burdensome, but very frail. Why, it was as if I had been given a thin-shelled pullet's egg to carry on my palm from Equatorial Africa to Hoboken. Yes, she became for me, as it were, the subject of a bet—the trophy of an athlete's achievement, a parsley crown that is the symbol of his chastity, his soberness, his abstentions, and of his inflexible will.

And of Maisie Maidan, he observes:

Why, even I, at this distance of time, am aware that I am a little in love with her memory. I can't help smiling when I think suddenly of her—as you might at the thought of something wrapped carefully away in lavender, in some drawer, in some old house that you have long left.

Of his feeling when Leonora for the first time, as he puts it, paid any attention to his existence, he writes: 'She gave me, suddenly, yet deliberately, one long stare. . . . And it was a most remarkable, a most moving glance, as if for a moment a lighthouse had looked at me.' The rightness of this extraordinary image for its purpose is stunning. That is precisely how the impact of a hard, coldly integrated personality like Leonora's would feel to a tremulous soul like Dowell's. At a more intense moment, as when the leagued Leonora and Nancy are daily censuring Edward, the images may literally become lacerating.

> Those two women pursued that poor devil and flayed the skin off him as if they had done it with whips. I tell you his mind bled almost visibly. I seem to see him stand, naked to the waist, his forearms shielding his eyes, and flesh hanging from him in rags. I tell you that is no exaggeration of what I feel.

At times Dowell's quest to image a feeling is baffled, and his struggle for a form is brought to our conscious attention. Of a crucial scene between the couples, when the relationship between Florence and Edward is faintly emerging, he writes: 'I was aware of something treacherous, something frightful, something evil in the day. I can't define it and can't find a simile for it. It wasn't as if a snake had looked out of a hole. No, it was as if my heart had missed a beat. It was as if we were going to run and cry out; all four of us in separate directions, averting our heads.'

And on another occasion, when he is introducing Leonora, he attempts a peculiar image of the way Leonora looked in an evening dress. Not well, he thought, because it was always black, cleanly cut, and had no ruffling; her shoulders were too classical for it. 'She seemed to stand out of her corsage as a white marble bust might out of a black Wedgwood vase.' His own awareness of the strangeness of the image is indicated by the sentence that follows and closes the paragraph: 'I don't know'. As if to say, it is at least a try. His meaning is not so vague, however, and is reinforced by a more obvious image in the next paragraph when he observes that although he always loved Leonora, he had never had any sexual feeling toward her:

As far as I am concerned I think it was those white shoulders that did it. I seemed to feel when I looked at them that, if ever I should press my lips upon them, they would be slightly cold—not icily, not without a touch of human heat, but, as they say of baths, with the chill off. I seemed to feel chilled at the end of my lips when I looked at her. ...

In short, there was little of femininity about Edward's wife. In so many words, however, this is never said, not even in the expressive sentence which follows: 'No, Leonora always appeared to be at her best in a blue tailor-made.'

These examples are, by and large, bold and self-aware. Dowell is the conscious imagist trying to find forms for his experience. But the function of other images is subtler, more a part of the general emotional atmosphere. As an example we may take the second paragraph of Chapter Two, in which the dominant mood of the novel must still be established. Perplexed as to how to narrate his story, Dowell writes:

> I shall just imagine myself for a fortnight or so at one side of the fireplace of a country cottage, with a sympathetic soul opposite me. And I shall go on talking, in a low voice while the sea sounds in the distance and overhead the great black flood of wind polishes the bright stars. From time to time we shall get up and go to the door and look out at the great moon and say: 'Why, it is nearly as bright as in Provence!' And then we shall come back to the fireside, with just the touch of a sigh because we are not in that Provence where even the saddest stories are gay. Consider the lamentable history of Peire Vidal. Two years ago Florence and I motored from Biarritz to Las Tours, which is in the Black Mountains. In the middle of a tortuous valley there rises up an immense pinnacle and on the pinnacle are four castles —Las Tours, the Towers. And the immense mistral blew down that valley which was the way from France into Provence so that the silver-grey olive leaves appeared like hair flying in the wind, and the tufts of rosemary crept into the iron rocks that they might not be torn up by the roots.

In this paragraph Ford is both summing up in juxtaposed images the emotional dimensions of the novel and shaping the reader's responses and expectations. There is the warm, reassuring fireplace set, however, in the vast elemental context of the sea, the wind, and the stars; the moon which is not the soft, comforting moon of romance (this will not be that story); the sudden, by no means accidental, introduction of the 'lamentable' story of Peire Vidal; and the shift to the motoring trip to Las Tours, with all its wracking emotive diction: *Black Moun-*

tains; tortuous valley; immense mistral blowing down that valley (the earlier wind grown savage); *olive leaves like hair flying in the wind* (in the classic image of grief); and, finally, moving imagistically to the ultimate condition of the characters themselves, *the tufts of rosemary* (the name of no other flower, with its suggestion of love, purity and tenderness, could have been more appropriately selected) *crept into the iron rocks that they might not be torn up by the roots*. A paragraph which has begun in comparative calm ends with great violence, and the reader's readiness for the cruel story before him is by so much more prepared.

Still more subtle kinds of imagery emotionally pave the way for a fact or a response. In describing the slowness at first of his courtship of Florence, Dowell observes: 'Perhaps that was because it took place almost entirely during the daytime, on hot afternoons, when the clouds of dust hung like fog, right up as high as the tops of the thin-leaved elms. The night, I believe, is the proper season for the gentle feats of love, not a Connecticut July afternoon, when any sort of proximity is an almost appalling thought.' A key sentence in the next paragraph, dealing with Florence's preferences in a husband, explains the emotive purpose of this passage: 'And—she faintly hinted—she did not want much physical passion in the affair.' Even more subtle yet are those images which vivify a place and, by extension, a character. An exquisite example is the candle shades in Edward's study. Their greenness is reflected in the glass of his bookcases, and his face is always seen when he is there by the light in their openings. As a result, the room conveys the feeling of being suffused in a green coolness, as though it provided for him a kind of sanctuary, a place of refuge and meaning in a world otherwise searing. It is almost as though Ford had peculiarly in mind, so that it came out an imagistic pun, Marvell's 'green thoughts in a green shade'.

But if the poet Dowell draws heavily on the emotional resources of imagery, he does not neglect the power of allusion to shape and prepare feeling. Thus he frequently mentions the Protestant leader, Ludwig the Courageous, who 'wanted to have three wives at once—in which he differed from Henry VIII, who wanted them one after the other, and this caused a good deal of trouble'. The reference is significant both as preparation for the story of Edward and for the establishment of the religious conflict which shortly follows. Classical myth also is evoked by Dowell when he writes near the end: 'I seem to see poor Edward,

naked and reclining amidst darkness, upon cold rocks, like one of the
ancient Greek damned, in Tartarus or wherever it was.' Similarly, the
Hebraic-Christian myth of the Garden of Eden is suggested, though
never overtly, in the brilliant scene when Edward is falling in love with
Nancy while Florence looks on. The powerful effect is that of a blessed
Adam and Eve spied upon with passionate envy by the serpent.

One of the key emotive methods used by Ford in *The Good Soldier*
is the device of setting side by side details which do not naturally
connect, and thus compelling in the reader an imaginative, poetic leap
and resolution between them. Such effective juxtaposition can be seen
in Chapter Two, for example, in Dowell's apparently aimless but
decidedly meaningful shift from discussing the character of Florence
to telling the Provencal story of the troubador Peire Vidal and the
crucial part played in it by La Louve, the heartless She-Wolf. In a
similar way the gray-faced head-waiter of the hotel at Nauheim is
juxtaposed with Edward. When Leonora wishes to appropriate a table
reserved for others, the waiter objects. Although he knows that the
Ashburnhams would give him much less trouble and tip him far more
handsomely than the legitimate table-holders, he is intent on doing his
steadfast duty, which is the right and just thing. The notion of honor is
thus subtly introduced, and the waiter's code is an analogue of Edward's.

In managing prose rhythm to help achieve his emotive ends, Ford
demonstrates the utmost mastery. Economical and simple in diction,
unpretentious in sentence structure, his language moves through an
intricacy of cadences which richly but unobtrusively supports the
complexity of thought and feeling. Conversational in tone, it is yet a
prose which is as tightly drawn as can be imagined—a fact which
becomes clearer on subsequent readings of the novel. Probably Ford's
most striking rhythmic device is the effect of finality with which many
paragraphs end. After moving appropriately through a series of
sentences, the line of thought will suddenly be thrust into place in the
concluding statement—like a bolt shooting home. Most often the
thrust is ironic, like 'Well, I suppose she deserved all she got'. At other
times it will be a statement which has an impact because of revelation,
surprise, or shock: 'And, by God, she gave him hell'. 'Outside the
winter rain fell and fell. And suddenly [Nancy] thought that Edward
might marry someone else; and she nearly screamed.' In the closing,
most intense, section of the novel, no paragraph lacks its final jolt—in

sensibility as though one's heart were being struck at again and again. Together with the tight control of the prose itself, the effect achieves an extraordinary feeling of constant pressure.

But in rendering emotion, Ford does not employ oblique means only. At the most intense moments he can be powerfully direct. Perhaps no word occurs more frequently in *The Good Soldier*, for example, than agony and its forms. It is, in fact, the emblem of the work. Or consider such direct statements of the situation as:

> are all men's lives like the lives of us good people—like the lives of the Ashburnhams, of the Dowells, of the Ruffords—broken, tumultuous, agonized, and unromantic lives, periods punctuated by screams, by imbecilities, by deaths, by agonies?

Or, again, Dowell's explanation of why a man must go to the woman he loves for renewal of his courage and solution of his difficulties: 'We are all so afraid, we are all so alone, we all so need from the outside the assurance of our own worthiness to exist.'

The technical importance of Dowell in shaping the responses of the reader is not confined, however, to various poetic, ironic, and stylistic elements. He also enables Ford brilliantly to manage feelings by controlling the tempo and tension of the novel and the degree of its psychological penetration. The structure of *The Good Soldier*, as a result, is extraordinary in its gripping suspense, narrative drive, and emotional concentration.

The use of Dowell to bridge time, which we noted earlier, may now be examined more closely. Ford's problem was not unlike one James faced in writing a famous tale in which he wanted to present the spiritual changes in a young woman over a considerable period. To do this he selected a narrator who reports his encounters with her on four separate, revealing occasions, hence the story's title, 'The Four Meetings'. In his book on James, published not long before his novel, Ford took special note of this tale by devoting three pages of discussion to it (including this sentence which seems particularly appropriate to Dowell: 'Mr James knows very well that he was giving just an extra turn to the tragedy of the story by making his narrator so abnormally unhelpful.') And in one important respect, the story would seem to have served as his technical model, for Ford focuses the action around three specific encounters among his characters. Thus, although the chronicle of *The Good Soldier* spans many years, it concentrates on the inital meeting of the two couples at Nauheim; the death of Florence and Edward's discovery of his love for Nancy in the same place nine years later; and the two-month period which follows at Branshaw after the Ashburn-hams return to England. As a result the novel gains greatly in dramatic unity and immediacy. Unlike James, however, Ford is not limited to these major dramatic occasions. (It is partly the difference between the tale and the novel.) For, as we have seen, much of the book traces the careers, motivations, and actions of the characters in the periods before the couples meet and in the interval between the episodes. The reader becomes acquainted with them in full dimension, so that the crucial incidents take on considerable authority and depth. The important technical point, however, is that Dowell (or Ford) presents only the highlights of the 'justifying' actions. One of the most unusual features of the novel in fact is that very few of its episodes last more than a page. A very important scene continues two pages, and only a few are longer. The novel has no lengthy exchanges of dialogue. In a scene of dramatic confrontation, the reader will be led up to the height of the incident; a character will speak an intense, key speech and may or may not be answered; and the episode is finished, its point burning like a brand into the reader's consciousness. Being extremely concentrated, the method wins for the book an emotional penetration rare in fiction.

This emotional penetration is, naturally, not attained only through concentrated impressions. It requires as well a plot development that will couple concentration with the highest degree of narrative tension, and this Ford achieves. The effect, as was said, is a series of surprises, brought about by new insights into facts and relationships—the constant turning of the screw.

Basically Ford uses the device of beginning in the midst of action. His tactic is to grip the reader's attention by presenting as forcefully as he can an emotional conflict at the peak of its intensity, and then, having aroused the desire to know more about it, to develop the background which led to the situation. His special skill is in so presenting the expository material that the tension is not quickly resolved, but keeps pulling the reader on and on. For these purposes Dowell is admirably contrived. His state of shock at what he has only recently discovered, together with his somewhat foolish, ineffectual character, goes far towards justifying the rambling method with which he tells the story. He himself is still in process; his personal attitudes towards the various other characters are not finally formed. As he begins to write, he does not even know the final outcome of the action: the closing two chapters, written on his return with Nancy from Ceylon, are completed months later. One probably need not add, however, that the ramblingness of the narrative is only seeming. 'Not one single thread must ever escape your purpose',[4] Ford always insisted, and none does in *The Good Soldier*.

Ford's success in intensifying the movement of his novel depends also on the skill with which in the opening chapters he keeps his basic emotional materials at several steps removed. Since the narrator himself so much fills the foreground at the beginning, the passionate emotions of the other characters, of which he is reporter, come to the reader only in isolated bursts—vivid but 'unplaced', and so muted in penetrative force. No less important in moderating the emotional power are Dowell's ironic tone, his indirection, and the abundant use of intellectual imagery. Later in the novel these screening elements begin to dissipate. The reader moves closer and closer to the characters, until their emotional responses are rendered with almost excruciating directness.

Among the most extraordinary of many extraordinary qualities about *The Good Soldier* is that although Ford has presented an account of drifting lives which, considered chronologically, fail to move towards any swift or inevitable end, he has nevertheless produced an artistic work which is singularly distinguished by its sense of swift inevitability. Ford's canons of economy and movement, to produce the sense of relentless destiny in a novel, are perfectly embodied in *The Good Soldier*. Every word is carefully chosen to advance the action; digressions relax tension, but are only seemingly digressions; the narrative moves faster and faster and with increasing intensity (*progression d'effet*). Finally the entire novel draws to one inevitable culmination, which, as Ford said, should reveal 'once and for all, in the last sentence, or the penultimate, in the last phrase or the one before it—the psychological significance of the whole.'[5] In *The Good Soldier* this culminating moment occurs one page from the end. All the facts of the story have been recorded, and the book seems to be trailing away without any final climax. Suddenly remembering, however, that he has not told how Edward met his death, Dowell depicts the scene at Branshaw

when Nancy's telegram arrived. Until this point in the novel the telegram has been several times referred to indirectly, and vaguely described
as 'atrocious'. Now Ford sets down the actual message, and its bright,
hard words provide the final turn of the screw, the ultimate clinching
cruelty. At one instant, and with a shock of perception, the reader
understands both why Edward had to end his life and why Nancy, on
learning of his suicide (and knowing its cause), had to go mad. In the
face of such cruelty in the human heart, withdrawal from life is the only
conceivable course for such sensitive beings. The reader has been
magnificently prepared to feel the horror of it. All forces have contributed to the inevitable end.

Finally, one further point of Ford's art ought not to be overlooked
—the size and depth given to the novel by its great number and
variety of marvelously executed scenes, each of which is a model of
artistry, with its own individual angle of attack, appropriate tone and
mood, structural rhythm and prose cadence. There are episodes, for
example, of social comedy: the two Hurlbird aunts in their Stamford
home (with its picture of General Braddock), delicately trying to warn
Dowell against their niece; the pathetic post-midnight elopement of
Dowell and Florence in Waterbury, Connecticut, and its aftermath:
the couple, 'listening to a mocking-bird imitate an old tom-cat' while
they dully wait in the woods for dawn; the photographing of Leonora
and her six sisters at their impoverished manor house and the other
hopeful expenditures made for the visit of the Ashburnhams and their
marriageable son; Edward at Monte Carlo with the Spanish dancer;
Leonora striking Maisie Maidan in a hotel corridor and her attempted
recapture of poise on discovering that Florence had been a witness; or
Dowell's fateful meeting with the odious Mr Bagshawe, who knew of
'Florrie' Hurlbird's affair with Jimmy. There are also the splendid
scenes of graver import: Dowell's almost stream-of-conscious memory
(a technique unusual in the book) of his catatonic state after Florence's
death; Dowell and Leonora in the dead-world of Branshaw after
Edward's suicide, with the rabbits already beginning to nibble the lawn;
the narrator's magnificent, extremely moving disquisition on the
growth and meaning of a man's love for a woman; the sequence,
purely quivering in its feeling, when the simple Nancy discovers
(through reading the newspapers) the existence of marital infidelity,
perceives the bitter hate between the Ashburnhams, and, with a sense

of age and wisdom and of superiority over Leonora, at once recognizes her own proud love for Edward; or the terrible scene at the end in which, with Dowell looking on, Edward and Nancy, those restrained 'good people' of England, bid each other goodbye at the railroad station without any sign of emotion. ('The signal for the train's departure was a very bright red', Dowell writes; 'that is about as passionate a statement as I can get into that scene.') Only a reader of the novel can understand the full variety and brilliance of such episodes, how admirably they have been selected to impel the action, or how masterfully they establish the breadth and solidity of the work.

The intense, complex experience of *The Good Soldier* and the means by which Ford successfully mounted it have by now been isolated. Still before us, however, is its larger significance. What, ultimately, is Ford saying in the novel? In his examination of character and of the agonies of human relationships the intention is apparent enough. But, like Flaubert, Ford does not express his full meaning obviously. Rather he subtly implies it, asking the reader to actively participate in understanding it. There are mysteries in *The Good Soldier* and the mind cannot rest until it resolves them.

Earlier the novel was described as a classic rendering of the modern tragic outlook. What was meant, more specifically, was that in it Ford has presented a genuinely tragic experience but in circumstances, peculiar to the twentieth century, which condition that experience in a special, meaningful way.

Those elements which make for the tragedy of the action are classically Aristotelian: its sense of inevitability, its reversals of situation and meaning, its high poetry. Its protagonist, Edward Ashburnham, is a man much above the ordinary. He lives according to the high values of generosity, kindness, duty, and responsibility to those who depend upon him, and he can act for the right with will and determination. 'The unfortunate Edward,' Dowell writes. 'Or, perhaps, he was not so unfortunate; because he had done what he knew to be the right thing, he may be deemed happy.' If Edward at his introduction seems, like Dowell, essentially a creation of comedy—an indulgent libertine, athletically handsome but basically stupid and vacuous—his dignity and stature steadily grow during the book until at its close he is an extremely impressive, noble figure. By no means a perfect man—the tragic protagonist never is—he is a good man who has never been guided by base motives. As Dowell makes clear, he was not a promiscuous libertine, but a sentimentalist. (In Mr Schorer's analysis, Edward is simply a libertine, having neither dignity nor depth and subject to the same distressingly hard scorn which marks the approach to Dowell. The reader would not even discern that Edward, not the narrator, is the central figure of the novel.) Sentimentality in fact is Edward's basic human weakness, his fatal flaw—even, as, ironically, it is the source of much of his virtues. Most importantly, *The Good Soldier* arouses in the reader the cathartic emotions of pity and awe at the spectacle of its admirable, greatly suffering protagonist overwhelmed by hard cruelty in so terrible and unfeeling a way.

These are the classic attributes of tragedy, but this experience is significantly qualified by elements that are not tragic. The sense of destiny, for example, is merely formal. The lives of the characters actually trail away to no seeming conclusion. Nor does the tragic experience of Edward and Nancy move in the larger context of a universe which is purposeful, either of the classical Greek determinism or the Hebraic-Christian Divine Plan. Instead Ford has placed the pair in a world in which, there being no purpose, there is hence no meaning to life on earth, only an ultimate knowledge of futility. At one place Dowell writes of himself and Leonora: 'I cannot tell you the extraordinary sense of leisure that we two seemed to have at the moment. It wasn't as if we were waiting for a train, it wasn't as if we were waiting for a meal—it was just that there was nothing to wait for. Nothing.' This motif of nothingness, which is actually announced in the opening chapter ('And there is nothing to guide us. . . . It is all a darkness.'), is re-sounded almost at the very end of the novel when Dowell presents his final description of the insane Nancy: 'It is very extraordinary to see the perfect flush of health on her cheeks, to see the lustre of her coiled black hair, the poise of the head upon the neck, the grace of the white hands—and to think that it all means nothing—that it is a picture without a meaning.'

The religious framework of the world, with its vision of harmony between God, man, and nature, has been shattered. This catastrophe and its consequences Ford crystallizes through brilliant juxtaposition in at least two key places in the novel. The first is the somewhat bathetic contrast (in the concluding chapter of Part One) between the powerful, compelling image of the palm of God and the comic, half-mocking and (half-weeping) image of the death and doll-like religious funeral of Maisie Maidan. More striking still, and more obvious in its meaning, is the conjunction of the only comments which are spoken by Nancy after she goes insane. 'Credo in unum Deum Omnipotentem' is the first, and about it Dowell sadly, wearily comments: 'Those are the only reasonable words she uttered; those are the only words, it appears, that she ever will utter. I suppose that they are reasonable words; it must be extraordinarily reasonable for her, if she can say that she believes in an Omnipotent Diety.' Almost at the end of the book Nancy speaks the other: a single word, repeated three times, 'Shuttlecocks'. That is how she felt between Leonora and Edward, and that was the way Edward had felt between the women. And that is the word, Ford is saying, for man's buffeted, purposeless existence in the world that has come into being.

We can now understand also the full ambiguity and subtlety of the scene in which, when Florence had disclosed a copy of Luther's Protest, Leonora cried out: 'Don't you see that that's the cause of the whole miserable affair; of the whole sorrow of the world? And of the eternal damnation of you and me and them. . . .' Her words, of course, are addressed essentially to the quietly meaningful touching by Florence of Edward's wrist. Although a staunch Roman Catholic, Leonora in reality is not a religious woman at all, operating rather according to the rigid code of the Church, to its letter rather than its spirit. Yet the reader does not yet know this fact and the words make their significant effect in his mind. By them Ford is saying that the rise of Protestantism, which symbolizes the entire modern, skeptical, fragmenting impulse, is the source of the destruction of the old consoling religious framework and the whole present sorrow of the world.

This sense of a nothingness at the heart of the universe can also be seen, of course, in the questionings of Hamlet and the rages of Lear. But the distance between Shakespeare's world, in which only chinks in the spiritual framework are spied, and our own period is great. As the modern era moves on into the time of the high prestige of science and Darwinism, the religious structure holds less and less power over the minds and actions of men. And with the change comes the disappearance of the heroic attitude. ('I am not Prince Hamlet,' declares Prufrock; and Dowell says of himself in heaven: 'Well, perhaps they will find me an elevator to run.') Gone also is the deep assurance that evil must, for all its ravages, be overcome. In *Lear* the disaster of the King and Cordelia is meliorated by the bitter deaths of Goneril and Regan. In *The Good Soldier* Edward and Nancy, who are the spiritual descendants of Lear and his youngest daughter, are destroyed, while Leonora, for whom the evil sisters are an essential prototype, triumphs without final punishment. In the rendering of man's spiritual plight in the twentieth century, *The Good Soldier* is thus a major artistic document, an objective correlative of its age.

This twentieth century world Ford represents specifically through various symbols. One is his selection of a pair of Americans as the peripheral characters to his tragedy. Ford conceived of his fictional Americans—as may be observed in his *An English Girl* (1907) and *A Call* (1910) and in his presentation of Mrs de Bray Pape in *The Last Post*—as unrooted creatures and, hence, as faint, ineffective personalities. Several times Dowell speaks of himself in these terms, and his wife he once calls a 'paper personality' who at her death dropped completely out of recollection. Florence is also characterized by her American busybody but mindless desire to bring 'a little light into the world'. This meddling, Dowell pointedly defines through a digressive anecdote about her uncle, who on his world tour took with him thousands of California oranges to give as 'little presents' to strangers. The absurdity of the venture is epitomized brilliantly in the following passage:

> When they were at North Cape, even, he saw on the horizon, poor dear thin man that he was, a lighthouse. 'Hello', says he to himself, 'these fellows must be very lonely. Let's take them some oranges.' So he had a boatload of his fruit out and had himself rowed to the lighthouse on the horizon.

'And so, guarded against his heart,' Dowell adds (in a double sense), 'and having his niece with him, he went round the world. . . .' This is the American in action, innocent of what lies below the surface of life, and often, as in the case of Dowell's wife, cheerfully doing evil.

Another meaningful symbol may be seen in Ford's depiction of Florence dead on her bed: 'looking with a puzzled expression at the electric-light bulb that hung from the ceiling, or perhaps through it, to the stars above'. Strikingly paralleling this description is a movement of Edward's just before he takes his life: 'He just looked up to the roof of the stable, as if he were looking to heaven . . .' We may note the contrast. For Edward, the agrarian stable (with its connotation even of the birth of Christ) and the searching appeal for heaven. For Florence, an electric light bulb, an almost by now classic symbol of the industrial substitution for Godhead, and the stars which coldly swing in the empty spaces above.

In dramatizing the nature of this dominant spirit, Ford did not rely, however, only on texture and subtly revealing incidents. He also built the point into the structure, so that the form itself defines and crystallizes its scope and large meaning; from beginning to end, its main action is transmitted through the sensibility of the narrator—an individual who brilliantly objectifies this lamed modern spirit. The ultimate importance (and final justification) of Dowell in the novel is as a concrete, functioning embodiment of the state of mind formed by the new conditions of the twentieth century world: alienated and unrooted, helpless and 'less than human', pathetic and absurd. As symbolic context, Dowell gives the tragedy a remarkably contemporary dimension. Ford has been praised for dramatizing in the Tietjens cycle the transition in England from one order of society to another, particularly in the composition of its governing classes, but in *The Good Soldier*, his *constatation* of change is still more penetrating. It is not limited to England, or its governing classes, or the public events of a decade. Rather it directly concerns itself, as we have noted, with a basic alteration that has steadily been going on in the attitudes and psychology of Western Man in general.

Having perceived the deeper significance of Ford's narrator, we must also consider the underlying meaning of his final fate. As owner of Branshaw Manor and as nursemaid to the mad Nancy, neither of which roles gives him any satisfaction, Dowell's end suggests a grim, sad prophecy. Ford appears to be saying by it that the modern estranged spirit, symbolized by Dowell in particular and Americans in general, will supplant the older types and values. (Edward, Nancy, and Branshaw, the seat of the stabler feudal attitudes based not on abstract capital but tangible land; even a Leonora.) Yet this spirit, being sick, will not be the possessor of the dying, blighted remains, but, like Dowell, their joyless caretaker.

Ford's story, in the end, however, focuses not on the ascendancy of the future, not on the 'new' man, but rather on the predicament and death of the old. Dowell (and Florence) are not, after all, at the center of the experience of *The Good Soldier*. That position is reserved for the

three English characters who move in the spiritual environment the
Americans represent. As personalities (and creations) they are in sharp
contrast with the Dowells, are strengthened and deepened by their
social, familial, and religious roots. They strive to put a face on life, to
give it meaning and purpose, to shore value, even if only sentimental,
against the ruins. None of them are personal ciphers, as modern writers
frequently have made their entrapped characters. If in a sense they
are victims, it is not in a simple reflex way, not the mere products of
society. In abundant measure they possess the will and passion to
victimize themselves. Their personal strength gives them their grandeur
and makes them worthy of such tragedy as Ford sees that the twentieth
century enables.

But in the end, of course, futility is the context in which they move.
Theirs is not the resolution finally of great tragedy, which in its heroism
confirms the optimistic view of man's ability to transcend himself
spiritually. Instead, for Edward and Nancy, it is the resolution of
withdrawal, by suicide and insanity, from a world which is too horrible.
Souls of a certain greatness have suffered greatly, but hopelessly and to
no larger purpose—their values, lacking sanction, are sentimental. This
is the tragic absurdity (or absurd tragedy) of human life in a world
bereft of meaning. The novel in every way earns its superlative claim.
It does, indeed, tell 'the saddest story'.

SOURCE: J. A. Meixner, *Ford Madox Ford's Novels* (1962).

NOTES

1. Ford Madox Ford, *Portraits from Life* (Boston, 1937) p. 217.
2. *The Kenyon Review*, II (spring 1949) 278.
3. *Henry James* (1913) p. 82.
4. *It Was the Nightingale* (Philadelphia and London, 1933) p. 212.
5. *Thus to Revisit* (1921) p. 44.

SAMUEL HYNES

The Epistemology of
The Good Soldier (1961)

THE problems involved in the interpretation of *The Good Soldier* all stem from one question: What are we to make of the novel's narrator? Or, to put it a bit more formally, what authority should we allow to the version of events which he narrates? The question is not, of course, particular to this novel; it raises a point of critical theory touching every novel which employs a limited mode of narration.

The point is really an epistemological one; for a novel is a version of the ways in which a man can know reality, as well as a version of reality itself. The techniques by which a novelist controls our contact with his fictional world, and particularly his choice of point of view and his treatment of time, combine to create a model of a theory of knowledge. Thus the narrative technique of Fielding, with the author omniscient and all consciousness equally open to him, implies eighteenth-century ideas of Reason, Order, and General Nature, while the modern inclination toward a restricted and subjective narrative mode implies a more limited and tentative conception of the way man knows.

When we speak of a limited-point-of-view novel, then, we are talking about a novel which implies a limited theory of knowledge. In this kind of novel, the reality that a man can know is two-fold; the external world exists as discrete, observed phenomena, and the individual consciousness exists. That is, a man is given what his senses tell him, and what he thinks. 'The central intelligence' is a narrow room, from which we the readers look out at the disorderly phenomena of experience. We do not *know* (as we know in Fielding) that what we see has meaning; if it has, it is an order which the narrator imposes upon phenomena, not one which is inherent there. And we can know only one consciousness—the one we are in. Other human beings are simply other events outside.

F.M.F.—4

This seems to be equally true of first- and third-person narration in this mode; it is difficult to see an epistemological difference between, say, *The Ambassadors* and *The Aspern Papers*. James, however, favored the third-person method, and used it in all his major novels. He did so, I think, because it enabled him to take for granted, 'by the general law of nature', as he put it, 'a primary author'; it allowed him, that is to say, to retain a vestige of authority, even though that authority 'works upon us most in fact by making us forget him'. In fact, though the 'primary author' of James's novels is a rather retiring figure, we do not forget him, and from time to time he comes forward to realign us with the truth, to tell us what we know.

In the first-person novel, on the other hand, it is at least possible to eliminate authority altogether, and to devise a narrative which raises uncertainty about the nature of truth and reality to the level of a structural principle. A classic example is the one before us, and it is in these terms that I will examine Ford's narrative techniques.

The Good Soldier is 'A Tale of Passion', a story of seduction, adultery, and suicide told by a deceived husband. These are melodramatic materials; yet the novel is not a melodrama, because the action of which it is an imitation is not the sequence of passionate gestures which in another novel we would call the plot, but rather the action of the narrator's mind as it gropes for the meaning, the reality of what has occurred. It is an interior action, taking its order from the processes of a puzzled mind rather than from the external forms of chronology and causation. This point is clear enough if one considers the way in which Ford treats the violent events which would, in a true melodrama, be climactic—the deaths of Maisie Maidan, Florence, and Ashburnham. All these climaxes are, dramatically speaking, 'thrown away', anticipated in casual remarks so as to deprive them of melodramatic force, and treated, when they do occur, almost as afterthoughts. (Ashburnham's death is literally an afterthought: Dowell says on the last page but one, 'It suddenly occurs to me that I have forgotten to say how Edward met his death', and even then he does not give us an account of the actual suicide.)

The narrative technique of *The Good Soldier* is a formal model of this interior action. We are entirely restricted to what Dowell perceives, and the order in which we receive his perceptions is the order of his thought; we never know more than he knows about his 'saddest story', and we must accept his contradictions and uncertainties as stages in our own progress toward knowledge. At first glance, Dowell seems peculiarly ill-equipped to tell this story, because he is ill-equipped to *know* a tale of passion. He is a kind of eunuch, a married virgin, a cuckold. He has apparently never felt passion—certainly he has never acted passionately. He is a stranger to human affairs; he tells his wife's aunts that he does nothing because he has never seen any call to. And he is an American, a stranger to the society in which his story takes place.

But more than all this, Dowell would seem to be disqualified as the narrator of *any* story by the doubt and uncertainty which are the defining characteristics of his mind. One phrase runs through his narrative, from the first pages to the last: 'I don't know'; and again and again he raises questions of knowledge, only to leave them unanswered: 'What does one know and why is one here?' 'Who in this world can know anything of any other heart—or of his own?'

The patent inadequacies of Dowell as a narrator have led critics of the novel to dismiss his version of the meaning of the events, and to look elsewhere for authority. Mark Schorer speaks of Dowell's 'distorted understanding', and James Hafley of his 'incoherent vision', and both look outside the narrator himself for objective truths to justify their judgments. But the point of technique here is simply that the factors which seem to disqualify Dowell—his ignorance, his inability to act, his profound doubt—are not seen in relation to any norm; there is neither a 'primary author' nor a 'knower' (of the kind of James's Fanny Assingham or Conrad's Marlow) in terms of which we can get a true perspective of either Dowell or the events of the novel. There is only Dowell, sitting down 'to puzzle out what I know'. The world of the novel is his world, in which 'it is all a darkness'; there is no knowledge offered, or even implied, which is superior to his own.

In a novel which postulates such severe limits to human knowledge —a novel of doubt, that is, in which the narrator's fallibility *is* the norm—the problem of authority cannot be settled directly, because the question which authority answers: 'How can we know what is true?' is itself what the novel is about. There are, however, two indirect ways in which a sense of the truth can be introduced into such a novel without violating its formal (which is to say epistemological) limitations: either through ironic tone, which will act to discredit the narrator's version of events and to imply the correctness of some alternative version, or through the development of the narrator toward some partial knowledge, if only of his own fallibility (and indeed in an extreme case this may be the only kind of knowledge possible for him). Glenway Wescott's *The Pilgrim Hawk* and Eudora Welty's 'Why I Live at the P. O.' are examples of the first device; each offers a sequence of events which are in themselves clear enough to the reader, and the irony lies in the disparity which we feel between the way the narrator understands these events and the way we understand them. The point made is thus a point of character, the revelation of a personal failure of perception.

The Great Gatsby is a fair example of the other sort. Fitzgerald's Nick Carraway learns as the action moves, and though he misunderstands and is surrounded by misunderstanding, in the end he knows something about himself, and about Gatsby, and about the world. The point made is a point of knowledge.

It has generally been assumed by Ford's commentators that *The Good Soldier* belongs to the class of *The Pilgrim Hawk*; but in fact it is closer to *Gatsby*. Ford's novel is, to be sure, as ironic as Wescott's, but with this difference; that Ford's narrator is conscious of the irony, and consciously turns it upon himself. When he describes his own inactions, or ventures an analysis of his own character—when he says 'I appeared to be like a woman or a solicitor', and describes himself as 'just as much of a sentimentalist' as Ashburnham—he is consciously self-deprecating, and thus blocks, as any conscious ironist does, the possibility of being charged with self-delusion. Schorer errs on this crucial point when he says that 'the author, while speaking through his simple, infatuated character, lets us know how to take his simplicity and his infatuation'. For the author does not speak—the novel has no 'primary author'; it is Dowell himself who says, in effect, 'I am simple and infatuated' (though there is irony in this, too; he is not all *that* simple).

The case for reading the novel as Schorer does, as a comedy of humor, is based on the enormity of Dowell's inadequacies. There are two arguments to be raised against this reading. First, Dowell's failures —his failure to act, his failure to understand the people around him, his failure to 'connect'—are shared by all the other characters in the novel, and thus would seem to constitute a generalization about the human condition rather than a moral state peculiar to him. Alienation, silence, loneliness, repression—these describe Ashburnham and Leonora and

Nancy, and even 'poor Florence' as well as they describe Dowell. Each character confronts his destiny alone.

Second, Dowell does have certain positive qualities which perhaps, in the light of recent criticism of the novel, require some rehabilitation. For instance, if his moral doubt prevents positive action, it also restrains him from passing judgment, even on those who have most wronged him. 'But what were they?' he asks. 'The just? The unjust? God knows! I think that the pair of them were only poor wretches creeping over this earth in the shadow of an eternal wrath. It is very terrible.' And though he doubts judgment—doubts, that is, the existence of moral absolutes—he is filled with a desire to know, a compelling need for the truth to sustain him in the ruin of his life. In the action of the novel, the doubt and the need to know are equally real, though they deny each other.

Dowell has one other quality, and it is his finest and most saving attribute—his capacity for love; for ironically, it is he, the eunuch, who is the Lover. Florence and Ashburnham and Maisie Maidan suffer from 'hearts', but Dowell is sound, and able, after his fashion, to love—to love Ashburnham and Nancy, and even Leonora. It is he who performs the two acts of wholly unselfish love in the book—he crosses the Atlantic in answer to Ashburnham's plea for help, and he travels to Ceylon to bring back the mad Nancy, when Leonora will not. And he can forgive, as no other character can.

This is the character, then, through whom Ford chooses to tell this 'saddest story'. He is a limited, fallible man, but the novel is not a study of his particular limitations; it is rather a study of the difficulties which man's nature and the world's put in the way of his will to know. Absolute truth and objective judgment are not possible; experience is a darkness, and other hearts are closed to us. If man nevertheless desires to know, and he does, then he will have to do the best he can with the shabby equipment which life offers him, and to be content with small and tentative achievements.

Dowell's account of this affair is told, as all first-person narratives must be, in retrospect, but the technique is in some ways unusual. We know the physical, melodramatic world only at one remove, so that the real events of the novel are Dowell's thoughts about what has happened, and not the happenings themselves. We are never thrown back into the stream of events, as we are, for example, in the narratives of

Conrad's Marlow; dramatic scenes are rare, and tend to be told in scattered fragments, as Dowell reverts to them in his thoughts. We are always with Dowell, after the event.

Yet though we are constantly reminded that all the events are over and done, we are also reminded that time passes during the telling (two years in all). The point of this device is the clear distinction that the novel makes between events and meaning, between what we have witnessed and what we know. All the returns are in, but their meaning can only be discovered (if at all) in time, by re-examination of the data, by reflection, and ultimately by love. And so Dowell tells his story as a puzzled man thinks—not in chronological order, but compulsively, going over the ground in circles, returning to crucial points, like someone looking for a lost object in a dim light. What he is looking for is the meaning of his experience.

Since the action of the novel is Dowell's struggle to understand, the events are ordered in relation to his developing knowledge, and are given importance in relation to what he learns from them. Thus we know in the first chapter that Dowell's wife, Florence, is dead, hear in the second chapter of Part II Dowell's account of that death (which he believes to be a heart attack), and only in Part III learn, through Dowell's account of Leonora's version of the event, that it was in fact suicide. We move among the events of the affair, to stand with Dowell for a moment behind Ashburnham, then to Leonora, to Nancy, and back to Ashburnham, getting in each case an account, colored always by Dowell's compassionate doubt, of the individual's version of events. The effect of this ordering is not that we finally see one version as right and another as wrong, but that we recognize an irresolvable pluralism of truths, in a world that remains essentially dark.

There are, as I have said, certain crucial points in the narrative to which Dowell returns, or around which the narrative hovers. These are the points at which the two conflicting principles of the novel—Convention and Passion—intersect. The most important of these is the 'Protest' scene, in which Florence shows Ashburnham the Protestant document, signed by Luther, Bucer and Zwingli, which has made him what he is—'honest, sober, industrious, provident, and clean-lived'. Leonora's reaction to this typical tourist scene strikes Dowell as a bit extravagant:

'Don't you see,' she said, with a really horrible bitterness, with a really horrible lamentation in her voice, 'Don't you see that that's the cause of the whole miserable affair; of the whole sorrow of the world? And of the eternal damnation of you and me and them. . . .'

He is relieved when she tells him that she is a Roman Catholic because it seems to provide an explanation of her outburst; and later his discovery that Florence was Ashburnham's mistress offers another, and more credible explanation. But neither explanation is really adequate. For Leonora is not simply reacting either to Protestantism or to adultery; she is reacting, in the name of a rigid conventionalism, to the destructive power of passion, which may equally well take the form of religious protest or of sexual license.

Ford once described himself as 'a sentimental Tory and a Roman Catholic', and it is in these two forms that convention functions in *The Good Soldier* (and in a number of his other novels as well). Society, as Dowell recognizes, depends on the arbitrary and unquestioning acceptance of 'the whole collection of rules'. Dowell is, at the beginning of his action, entirely conventional in this sense; conventions provide him with a way of existing in the world—they are the alternatives to the true reality which man cannot know, or which he cannot bear to know. From conventions he gets a spurious sense of permanence and stability and human intimacy, and the illusion of knowledge. When they collapse, he is left with nothing.

Leonora's conventions are her 'English Catholic conscience, her rigid principles, her coldness, even her very patience', conventions which are, Dowell thinks, 'all wrong in this special case' (it is characteristic of him that he refuses to generalize beyond the special case). Ashburnham's are those of a sentimental Tory—'what was demanded by convention and the traditions of his house'. (A first draft of Ashburnham appears in *The Spirit of the People*, Ford's study of the English mind; there the scene between Ashburnham and Nancy at the railway station is offered as an example of the Englishman's characteristic reticence and fear of emotion.) It is by these conventions that the husband and wife act at crucial moments; but it is not conventions alone which bring about their tragedy. It is, rather, the interaction of Convention and Passion.

Passion is the necessary antagonist of Convention, the protest of the individual against the rules. It is anarchic and destructive; it reveals the secrets of the heart which convention exists to conceal and repress; it knows no rules except its own necessity. Passion is, of course, an ambiguous term. To the secular mind it is likely to suggest simply sexual desire. But it also means suffering, and specifically Christ's sacrificial suffering. I don't mean to suggest that Ashburnham is what it has become fashionable to call a 'Christ-figure'—I dislike the critical method which consists in re-writing novels as Passion Plays—but simply that the passionate sufferings of Ashburnham (and even of Leonora) are acts of love, and as such have their positive aspects. Convention, as Dowell learns, provides no medium for the expression of such love. In conventional terms it is true, as Dowell says, that Edward and Nancy are the villains, and Leonora the heroine, but the expense of her conventional heroism is the defilement of what is best in her, and the destruction of what she loves, while the 'villains' are, in their suffering, blessed; the epigraph of the novel is their epitaph: *Beati Immaculati*, blessed are the pure.

Between the conflicting demands of Convention and Passion, the characters are, as Nancy says, shuttlecocks. 'Convention and traditions I suppose,' Dowell reflects near the end of the book, 'work blindly but surely for the preservation of the normal type; for the extinction of proud, resolute, and unusual individuals.' Passion works for the reverse.

In the action of Dowell's knowing, he learns the reality of Passion, but he also acknowledges that Convention will triumph, because it must. 'Society must go on, I suppose, and society can only exist if the normal, if the virtuous, the slightly deceitful flourish, and if the passionate, the headstrong, and the too-truthful are condemned to suicide and to madness.' Yet in the end he identifies himself unconditionally with Passion: 'I loved Edward Ashburnham,' he says, 'because he was just myself.' This seems a bizarre assertion, that Dowell, the Philadelphia eunuch, should identify himself with Ashburnham, the English country squire and lover ('this is his weirdest absurdity,' Schorer remarks of this passage, 'the final, total blindness of infatuation, and self-infatuation'). But in the action of the novel the identification is understandable enough. The problem that the novel sets is the problem of knowledge, and specifically knowledge of the human heart: 'Who in this world knows anything of any other heart—or of his own?' Dowell, in the end, *does* know another human heart—Ashburnham's, and knowing that heart, he knows his own. By entering selflessly into another man's suffering, he has identified himself with him, and identity is knowledge. He is, to be sure, ill-equipped for this knowledge; he lacks, as he says, Ashburnham's courage and virility and physique—everything, one would think, that goes to make an Ashburnham. But by an act of perfect sympathy he has known what Ashburnham was, and he can therefore place himself honestly in the category of 'the passionate, of the headstrong, and the too-truthful'.

With this confession, the affair is over. The action in Dowell's mind is complete, or as complete as it can be in a novel built on doubt. The repeated questions, which Ford uses as Shakespeare uses questions in the tragedies, almost as symbols of the difficulty of knowing, disappear from the last chapter; but they are replaced, not by an emergent certainty, but by resigned admissions of the limits of human knowledge: 'I don't know. I know nothing. I am very tired' and 'I can't make out which of them was right. I leave it to you.' To know what you can't know is nevertheless a kind of knowledge, and a kind that Dowell did not have at the beginning of the affair. Of positive knowledge, he has this: he knows something of another human heart, and something also of the necessary and irreconcilable conflict which exists between Passion and Convention, and which he accepts as in the nature of things. Beyond that, it is all a darkness, as it was.

SOURCE: *Sewanee Review*, LXIX (spring 1961).

JO-ANN BAERNSTEIN

Image, Identity, and Insight in
The Good Soldier (1966)

IN a search to find some way to extricate the 'objective reality' of the events narrated from the controlling and seemingly distorted intelligence of the narrator of *The Good Soldier* some critics have gone so far as to say that 'whether Ford intended the events of *The Good Soldier* to have some objective reality or not, all the events as they appear in this novel must be influenced by the intelligence of Dowell'.[1] Other critics, taking a more moderate view, have found some indirect means by which a 'sense of the truth can be introduced into such a novel without violating its formal limitations'.[2] Hynes, in his article 'The Epistemology of *The Good Soldier*', gives two instances of indirect means as an 'ironic tone' which will not only undercut the narrator's view but which will also imply a correct one, and, as a development of the narrator toward a knowledge with which he did not begin.[3] Although we cannot separate the narrator's intelligence and possible distortion of the events as given from the 'actual' or 'factual' event, we can try to find a mode of his perception of other characters and events of which he seems to be unaware. If this can be found without violating the controlling structure of the narrative, then it is possible to cite a sustained, ironic motif which will yield a different view of the narrator himself. This sustained motif is found in Dowell's abundant use of animal images throughout the novel and his apparent ignorance of the themes presented through them. These themes are of disguise and the transference of male and female roles in a context of animal imagery, and through them we can postulate a second level of meaning implicit in Dowell's statement of identity with Ashburnham which seems to come as such a 'comic shock' at the end of the novel.

This use of animal imagery appears to have been a habit of mind of Ford himself. When Ford describes his work in his own terms, in his introductory dedication of *The Good Soldier*,[4] strangely enough, he uses some of the same imagery with which Dowell, his narrator, reveals, inadvertently, another level of meaning in his experience. Before writing *The Good Soldier*, Ford says, he has never tried to improve on his previous efforts; he had never attempted to 'extend' himself. This phrase, from 'race-horse training', is followed by Ford's metaphor for the creation and existence of his novel:

> So I regarded myself as the Eel which, having reached the deep sea, brings forth its young and dies—or as the Great Auk I considered that, having reached my allotted, I had laid my one egg and might as well die. So I took formal farewell of Literature in the columns of a magazine called the *Thrush* —which also, poor little auk that it was, died of the effort. (xix)

Ford says that, with this last effort, he was prepared to let the writers of a different generation take over. He continues his bird-egg imagery saying, 'so I have come out of my hole again and beside your strong, delicate, and beautiful works have taken heart to lay some work of my own'. Still, Ford says that *The Good Soldier* is his 'great auk's egg' because it is 'something of a race that will have no successors'. The idea had been 'hatching' in him for more than ten years and he had 'carried it about' since it could not be written until the 'real characters were all dead'. As he looks back over his book, marveling at his past ability, he thinks of himself as 'an extinct volcano'.

The obvious point to be made here is that Ford seems to see the writing and creation of the novel in about the same light that Dowell visualizes a major part of his experience. As Dowell carries his pullet's egg from Africa to Hoboken (91), so Ford carried the embryonic egg of *The Good Soldier* 'hatching' in him for years. Ford's great auk's egg, like Dowell's pullet's egg, is the last product of an extinct line, but Ford, unlike Dowell, was able 'to lay' again, create again. In contrast, his sterile narrator, while he resembles Ford, is left at the end of the novel in a position which denies fertility or the continuation of society. Dowell abhors the 'rabbits' of society and retreats from such demands. So, it seems, Ford was ready to retreat from his milieu and let the other writers take over. Ford makes use of the same symbolic transference of male and female roles, seeing himself as the egg-carrier, the egg-bearer, the female parent. Dowell, as the egg-bearer, is the wife in his marriage, but instead of gaining awareness and changing, he merely succeeds in duplicating his original position as nurse. Ford, far from

impotently retreating, is, even in his female role as creator, a fruitful
auk who becomes curiously like a phoenix. Dying after his last creative
effort, Ford rose again to the same level of creativity, out of the ashes
of the work of an extinct generation to produce in a new era.

In other words, I think the dedication to *The Good Soldier*, in certain
respects, serves as a cue to the habit of mind by which Ford creates the
second level implicit in Dowell's animal imagery. It reflects his narrator's
unknowing role transference while, at the same time, it denies im-
potence as a necessary outcome of such a reversal by the very fact of
creation which is Ford's novel. Whether or not Ford intended to give
his readers such cues to Dowell's habit of mind, his critics have noted
the way in which Dowell uses figurative language and juxtaposes
disparate details as a device to make his readers arrive at some conclusion.[5] Other critics have categorized the kinds of imagery Dowell
uses and have pointed out its relevance to Dowell's limited knowledge
of the world,[6] but so far no one has pointed out the fact that while
Dowell, in some cases, is consciously and painfully trying to find
metaphors for his experience, he is also, inadvertently, giving his
readers a cue to a dimension of his experience unknown to him.

The pattern of this imagery and the extent to which Dowell is aware
or ignorant of the pattern's meaning, as well as the difference his awareness or ignorance will make to an interpretation of the novel, can be
determined first by our understanding Dowell's conscious use of animal
images, and second by our finding the meaning that lies below his
conscious use of this imagery. We need to inquire not into what
actually occurred, but into Dowell's method of perception. We will ask
why he chose to use a particular detail of animal imagery, what aspect
of it embodies his explicit meaning, and what aspect embodies cues to
the implicit, sustained motif of his imagery. By this means we can find
an angle of vision on Dowell's narrative role and mode of perception of
which he, himself, seems to be ignorant. If we can determine, then, the
extent of Dowell's consciousness in his manipulation of animal imagery
throughout the novel, we may be able to go beyond (or below) the
distorting eye of the narrator to a less conceptual and confusing view of
the events and Dowell's perceptions in relation to them as the controlling intelligence.

Through his use of animal imagery in characterizing and in com-
municating some quality or idea of a person or event, groping for

visual ways to fix tone and verbalize an emotion, Dowell reveals the ways in which he consciously manipulates language throughout the novel. However, through specific and recurrent animal images, whether explicit or implied, Dowell employs a method of selection to focus his attempts at characterization. Dowell's mode of perception through animal imagery can be limited to three separate categories: (1) assuming it is his habit of mind to perceive in animal terms, we find he uses images which naturally correspond to the habits of his characters; (2) he reports, with no seeming connection to the narrative, what he sees 'out there'; (3) he uses animal imagery of his own invention to explain, consciously or not, the feeling quality of an emotion or experience. His focus on Edward, his explanations of Edward's sexual or social affairs, is in terms of horse imagery. To characterize his own actions or functions, Dowell uses, for the most part, dog images. His most ironic use of animal imagery is to characterize his wife Florence, who is surrounded by poultry images which serve as a comment on her maiden name, Hurlbird. Leonora, who is only portrayed in terms of animals towards the end of the novel, is initially seen by Dowell as a horsewoman, a rider or manager of horses. Swan imagery is used for both Maisie Maidan and Nancy Rufford but Nancy, as the novel progresses, is seen more and more in terms of dog images. The major portion of the animal imagery, then, is focused upon horses, dogs and birds, or poultry. The actions which correspond to these animals become the implied metaphors for the actions of the characters in the hunt, sports (polo) and the relationships between the rider and mount, the hunter and hunted, the predator and prey.

We will first examine the ways in which Dowell uses this imagery to characterize and describe action and then trace the ways in which his imagery progresses and changes to reflect changing action or awareness. In this way we can come to an understanding of the sustained motif, the themes and identities, of which Dowell is unaware.

Dowell, at the outset, connects horse imagery with sexuality and 'the heart'. 'Captain Ashburnham also had a heart . . . the reason for his heart was, approximately, polo, or too much hard sportsmanship in his youth' (4). As Dowell continues to describe Ashburnham and his actions, he uses horses and polo. On describing the 'purity' of Edward's mind and the 'chastity of his expressions' (11), Dowell is bewildered by the fact that these very elements of Edward's character, which he

himself shared, were 'the hall-mark of a libertine' (11), of 'a raging
stallion forever neighing after his neighbour's womankind' (12). Trying
to fix Edward's facial expression when they first meet, Dowell relates
an anecdote in which Edward had the same expression. Dowell,
characteristically, seems to see Edward and his horse as one, as he
describes the polo match in which Edward was able to gain a particularly difficult goal:

> The German Captain . . . was right up by their goal posts, coming with the
> ball in an easy canter in that tricky German fashion. The rest of the field
> were just anywhere. It was only a scratch sort of affair. Ashburnham was
> quite close to the rails not five yards from us and I heard him saying to
> himself: 'Might just be done!' And he did it. Goodness! He swung that
> pony around with all its four legs spread out, like a cat jumping off a roof.
> . . . Well, it was just that look that I noticed in his eyes: 'It might,' I seem
> even now to hear him muttering to himself, 'just be done.' I looked over
> my shoulder and saw . . . Leonora. And my . . . wife. (29–30)

Dowell connects the 'look' on Edward's face with his possession of
Branshaw and, later, with his sexual prowess. He says that, 'In the case
of the other women, Edward just cut in and cut them out as he did with
the polo-ball from under the nose of Count Baron von Lelöffel' (116).
As Dowell continues to narrate his meeting with the Ashburnhams, he
continues his riding imagery from the polo story, describing Leonora's
hesitation to join them as 'a quick sharp motion . . . as if her horse had
checked. But she put it at the fence all right, rising from the seat she had
taken and sitting down opposite me, as it were, all in one motion'
(31–2). As Edward is on the rails but turns his horse in a single motion,
so Leonora enters the company of Dowell. As if to complete, but
distinguish between, the kinds of horsemanship evidenced in Edward
and Leonora, Dowell proceeds to describe Leonora's facial expression
at their first meeting. 'I seemed to hear the brain ask and the eyes
answer with all the simpleness of a woman who was a good hand at
taking in qualities of a horse—as indeed she was. "Stands well; has
plenty of room for his oats. . . . Is this man trustworthy in money
matters; is he likely to play the lover; is he likely to let his women be
troublesome? Is he, above all, likely to babble about my affairs?" ' (33)
Leonora's handling of horses is in terms of 'checking' and 'reigning in',
to find if she can control the mount. Edward's horsemanship is, unlike
Leonora's, one of 'cutting out and carrying off' even in tight situations.

His concern is with possession, with the winning of a point, not with restraining or checking the motions of his mount.

In one of the few situations in which the characters are seen as a social unit rather than isolated individuals, this horse imagery plays an important part in their means of communication. Leonora, trying to control and check Florence's efforts to 'educate' Edward, says that she left Edward 'uninformed' because she had 'an idea that it might injure his hand—the hand, you know, used in connection with horses' mouths' (39). Then Edward, with unknowing irony, asks Dowell if 'having too much in one's head would really interfere with one's quickness in polo' (40). He thinks that 'brainy Johnnies' show up rather poorly when they get 'on to four legs' (40). Brainy John Dowell, unaware of the sexual connotations, notices merely that Edward seemed to enjoy being 'educated' by Florence. Although Leonora is ironically equating Florence's education of Edward with his physical treatment of horses in a sexual context, neither Edward nor Dowell recognize the intent of her remarks. Leonora, who is 'so splendid in the saddle' (8), snorts in contempt (46) upon discovering Florence's purposes in educating Edward but it is she who 'had him prancing around . . . on a thousand dollar horse with the gladdest of glad rags all over him' (168). Throughout Dowell's use of this animal imagery to describe Edward and Leonora, the major portion of the recurrent horse images describe the sexual and social identity of Edward, while the metaphors of the rider and trainer are used as an ironic preview of their marriage.

A progressive changing and molding occurs in Dowell's use of animal imagery as his characterization of Leonora changes from horsewoman to stalking cat, from savage, hungry dog to a kind of rabbit. Edward follows a similar decline from 'raging stallion' to dumb hunted brute. As the emotional decline in the characters becomes more apparent, Dowell manipulates the imagery to mark this descent.

To Dowell, Leonora is first a relentless rider leashing in or driving, as best she can, a 'raging stallion'. Her 'riding' implies both the economic and sexual aspects of her actions in that Leonora managed both for Edward, who was struck by the fact that 'Leonora must be intending to manage his loves as she managed his money affairs' (174). Dowell described Leonora's view of Edward's affairs as 'rutting seasons' (186), but to keep their marriage together, she will allow the 'stallion' even more financial and sexual freedom: 'Yes, Leonora seemed to have got hold of the clue to the riddle. . . . She shoud not have kept Edward on such a tight rein with regard to money' (188). In effect, Leonora has been 'husbanding' Edward's property and women. In this context, Leonora's action concerning the 'affair' of Edward and Nancy Rufford was initially an effort to control them when she began 'to put the leash upon' them (123). When she begins to 'slacken' her control, to loosen the reins of their affair, she begins to deteriorate emotionally. 'And then, with the slackening of her vigilance, came the slackening of her entire mind,' says Dowell (134). Leonora, like her father, thought 'that Edward was riding hot-foot to ruin' (144) and she tried 'to rule with a rod of iron' (149) but, upon slackening the reins on Edward, she assumed a more destructive means of control. 'She would have liked to bring her riding-whip down across' Nancy's face (210) and 'she was lashing, like a cold fiend, into the unfortunate Edward' (211). Dowell explains that Leonora really 'lashed' into Edward more than she meant to do just because 'he was so silent' (213).

It is Leonora, Dowell tells us, who first compares herself to a cat. She watches Edward 'as a fierce cat watches an unconscious pigeon in the roadway' (130). Dowell takes up this image again to describe Leonora 'watching Edward more intently and with more straining of ears than that which a cat bestows upon a bird overhead' (178). In this way, Dowell says, Leonora watched the course of Edward's secret passions. By far the worst light in which he pictures Leonora is in her relationship to Edward and Nancy. Dowell imagines Nancy seeing Leonora as 'a hungry dog, trying to spring up at a lamb' (228-9), explaining that Nancy felt 'as if Edward's love were a precious lamb that she was bearing away from a cruel and predatory beast'. He goes on to say that 'Leonora with her hunger, with her cruelty, had driven Edward to madness' (229). As Leonora reveals the course of Edward's infidelities to Nancy, they both assume the role of hungry, savage dogs in their mutual pursuit of Edward. In a scene reminiscent of the Vidal story, Dowell describes them as having 'pursued that poor devil and flayed the skin off him as if they had done it with whips' (239). And this affects Dowell so greatly that he imagines seeing Edward standing 'naked to the waist, his forearms shielding his eyes, and flesh hanging from him in rags' (239).

Edward's decline parallels Leonora's deterioration as he gradually loses his identity with horses and becomes a beaten, silent brute. In direct contrast to Mr Basil, who collects 'restraining bits', and to Leonora, who, like Mr Basil, tries to restrain Edward financially through manipulation of his affairs (165), Edward invents a new stirrup which he then presents to the army (195). Edward's effort, which infuriates Leonora, seems a symbolic last-ditch attempt to retain his mount, to secure his position, but he not only gives away the stirrup, he also gives up the horse. He makes a gift of his 'old, Irish cob' to a young boy whose father has been financially ruined (208). If we consider these two 'gifts', we see Edward giving away his identity as soldier and gentleman. Leonora controls his finances and, in relation to his virility, he is no longer 'in the saddle', no longer 'a good soldier to a lady'.[7]

Edward's giving away the Irish cob is the temporal action which marks the beginning of Nancy's change, not only in mentality but also in the quality of the images with which she is described by Dowell. Before Leonora's account of his affairs, Nancy considered Edward to be 'a nice dog, a trustworthy horse or a girl friend' (207), and Leonora the predator (228–9). The two women, holding disparate opinions of Edward's merit, confront each other 'like beasts about to spring' (229).

Although there is an eighteen month break in his narrative, when Dowell takes up his story again, writing at Branshaw, where he nurses the mad Nancy, his use of images to complete the idea of the flaying of Edward by the two women, as if possessed of its own sequence, continues to follow the initial decline in animal bestiality. In other words, this time lapse, at least in terms of the gradual pejorative connotations of the animal imagery used to depict the decline of the characters from the outset, does not seem to affect the chronological series of images which embody the feeling quality of a growing savagery in the animals used to characterize the deterioration of the conditions, emotions and actions of his subjects.

Swayed by Leonora's accounts of his affairs, Nancy slowly begins to change her opinion of Edward and comes to see him, not Leonora, as the 'beast'. Leonora, Dowell tells us, makes Nancy believe that she had endured great torment and 'spoke of the agonies she had endured during her life with the man, who was violent, overbearing, vain, drunken, arrogant, and monstrously a prey to his sexual necessities' (241). The irony, in terms of the progression of animal imagery, is that by this point in the narrative Edward is prey, not to a monstrous lust, but

rather a prey of Leonora and, finally, Nancy. The parallel declines of
Edward's symbolic disintegration and the reduction of the women to
predators turning on Edward, meet in the scene in which Dowell describes the flaying of Edward. The steps in this imagined process are
outlined by Dowell, who recreates Leonora's lashing of Edward in the
gun-room where Edward is surrounded by the remnants of his previous
identity. Nancy, continually prompted by Leonora, finally confronts
Edward in his bedroom, but he orders her away 'as he would have done
to a servant or a horse' (243). This confrontation, to Dowell, is part of
the planned infliction of cruelty on Edward by both women who
'pursued that poor devil' (239). Dowell imagines Nancy initially
regarding Edward in the same way that Edward apparently regards
Dowell, 'as a trustworthy girl friend' (207) or as 'a woman and solicitor'
(249). In the same room in which Leonora began her lashing of
Edward, Edward begins his confession to Dowell that he loves Nancy
Rufford.

The last glimpse we have of Edward and Dowell together is in the
scene of the suicide in the stables. The symbolic setting for Edward's
death is reinforced by Dowell's mental association with, and almost
automatic assumption of, his role as 'trusty dog', as he 'trotted off' to
Leonora with the telegram-newspaper in his mouth while Edward,
looking up to the roof of the stable, cuts his throat. 'Leonora was quite
pleased with it,' Dowell remarks (256). In his recreation of the suicide,
Dowell uses implied animal images to create a symbolic setting and also
to set up the structural separation of the hearth and the stable. This
distinction between dog-hearth-domestic animal and horse-stable-wild
animal is the very one that Dowell uses to make himself 'in his fainter
way' (253) like Edward, in that they both 'have rushed through all
Provence—and all Provence no longer matters' (234).

In Dowell's conscious use of animal imagery, then, there is a progression, a downward movement in character and action, but, strangely,
Dowell's animal images to characterize himself, overtly, are not involved in any such transformation or change. If he has learned from his
experience, would this knowledge not be borne out in his imagery,
depicting, as he does with the others, the violent upheavals which,
in some way, change his life?

From the beginning, Dowell connects himself with the domestic,
trained and passive hearth-side animal, even as he curls up by his

imaginary fireplace to tell his story. As a 'sedulous, strained [trained?] nurse' (8) and guide-dog for Florence, Dowell, who thinks Leonora sees him as a 'clean bull-terrier' (31), had 'tracked off' (82) and married a heart patient, thereby spending the next twelve years 'playing the trained poodle' (120). After her death-suicide, Dowell explains his 'catalepsy' as the result of 'twelve years of the repression of [his] instinct' (120) but his immobile, unthinking state after her death is so close to the passive, impotent inaction of his marriage that it seems to be only an intensification of his previous twelve years. Unlike the horse imagery used to depict Edward's race for death, Dowell, explaining his reasons for not chasing Florence as she runs, white-faced, up to their room, uses this image: 'It would have been like chasing a scrap of paper' (121). In this race it would have been ignoble for a grown man to chase a scrap of paper like a playful dog but this is just how he pictures himself, at the end of the novel, trotting off to Leonora with a scrap of paper, a telegram. He implies that he might have gone up to Florence sooner and prevented her death had it not been for Bagshaw and, he implies at the end, that he did not wish to stop Edward's suicide either, although he knew what would happen. Is this evidence of awareness and compliance on Dowell's part or is it his paradoxical denial and acceptance of his role as 'trained dog', in one instance too warm by the fire to chase paper, in the other, too well trained not to? There may be a clue in Dowell's recurrent reference to Nancy Rufford and her St Bernard which will shed light on the nature of his awareness of the events which he describes. Dowell, trying to describe Nancy's dual nature, says that 'at one moment she would be talking of the lives of the saints and at the next she would be tumbling all over the lawn with the St Bernard puppy' (124). His very first mention of Nancy is of her 'being out with the hounds' (20) and if we remember Dowell's affinity for hearthsides in connection with his desire, on the night of Florence's suicide, to marry Nancy, we begin to see the St Bernard, Nancy's pet, in somewhat the same light in which Dowell visualizes himself. As he recreates the scenes of Nancy's growing awareness of adultery and the true nature of the Ashburnhams' marriage, Dowell describes, in counterpoise, the similar reactions of the St Bernard.

> The andirons with the brass flowers at the ends appeared unreal; the burning logs were just logs that were burning and not the comfortable symbols of an indestructible mode of life. The flame fluttered ... the St Bernard

sighed in his sleep ... Nancy said, 'I never imagined ... I thought you were married or not married as you are alive or dead.' 'That', Leonora said, 'is the law of the church. It is not the law of the land' ... 'Oh, yes,' Nancy said, 'the Brands are Protestants.' She felt a sudden safeness descend upon her ... the St Bernard awoke and lolloped away towards the kitchen ... She [Nancy] remembered that Edward's eyes were hopeless ... at times he sighed deeply ... Edward was a Protestant. Then Edward loved somebody ... her eyes grew hopeless; she sighed as the old St Bernard beside her did. (220–21, 224)

We have here, first, a recreation of the 'protest scene' (44–6) in which Leonora shielded Dowell from the incipient adultery by talking of Protestants and Catholics. Not to know the truth, to be warm by the hearthside, even if the logs are only logs; not to know that marriages disintegrate, to find a sense of security in the false distinctions of religion, even a false security, is just the way Dowell reacted to the 'protest' and is now the way he pictures Nancy's innocent reactions. In Dowell's recreation, the St Bernard sighs in his sleep at the threatened lack of security, leaves Nancy in her false security, and returns to sigh, as do Edward and Nancy, at the awareness that passion can be as hopeless as security, that things are not as they appear, that fire provides a false warmth but a real destructiveness. It seems that Dowell somehow projects his reactions into the sighing St Bernard and finds his awakening almost a counterpart to that of Nancy Rufford and her pet. It is in such an image as this that the reader can begin to see the transitional stage in the explicit and implicit meanings in Dowell's imagery.

Dowell, thus, makes a conscious effort to convey through this explicit use of animal imagery the unmasked identity of his characters, and the 'true' nature of their actions. The relationships indicated by the successive decline in types of animal metaphor and simile range from that of the functional horse-rider image to the isolated predator-prey. By using this device, Dowell penetrates the disguise of convention, to reveal the snarling, bestial nature of passions.[8]

On the surface, Dowell furnishes the reader with cues to the salient features of his animal analogies but he also establishes a latent substructure in which the animal imagery is an implicit and sustained motif below the level of his conscious narration. The actual unmasking by Dowell is really a prelude to another more revealing discovery, his identification with Edward Ashburnham. This identity is the result of an unconscious but recurrent transference of male and female roles in which the women are the aggressors, the husbands the cuckolds, and the men are the passive victims, the imitators, the wives. On this level the animal imagery serves to illuminate an almost dreamlike rendering of Dowell's desired identity, of sexuality vicariously experienced in a form which does not threaten him, which does not necessitate a physical demonstration of ability. It is the dream-vision of the trained poodle who thinks he wants to be a raging stallion.

In Part I, the structural basis for this reading is set up in three extended animal images which are picked up, in several contexts, throughout the remainder of the novel. In the Vidal story we have, in embryonic form, the idea of the transference of male and female roles, the aggressive woman, disguise, and Dowell's sexual identification with Edward. Traditionally, there is a 'jongleur' who sometimes sings the songs of his master, the troubador poet. He is a substitute, an apprentice to the poet and his title 'jongleur' denotes a juggler or deceiver who can verbally imitate the song of his master. This role of the 'jongleur', apprentice and juggler, fits Dowell, who tells this story and the main narrative as a juggler, as a faint substitute for Edward, who makes the song his own. The juggling of roles and the imitation of songs constantly recurs in the pattern of animal imagery.

Vidal, the poet, fails in his attempt to attract the already-married She-Wolf and, in tribute to his love, dresses himself in wolf-skins only to be torn apart by savage dogs mistaking him for the real thing. He is rescued by the husband of the She-Wolf, nursed back to health, and, then, declaring himself emperor of Jerusalem, goes on a crusade. The husband kisses Vidal's feet but the She-Wolf continues to ignore his antics. After another failure, Vidal is again rescued by the husband, whereupon he falls all over the She-Wolf's bed, only to be ignored again. The husband, who is a 'ferocious warrior', remonstrates with her, demanding for Vidal the proper courtesy due a great poet but, as Dowell remarks, 'I suppose La Louve was the more ferocious of the two' (16–17). This story can be juggled in relation to all the characters of the novel and illuminates, in essence, the idea that if the woman is the superior soldier, then the lover can only assume the disguise of the loved one and the husband can only assume the role of guide and nurse for the would-be adulterer. Edward's dual identity as soldier and sentimentalist are, in this story, divided between Vidal and the husband

of La Louve. The flaying of Vidal by the dogs recurs in Part IV in which
Dowell describes the flaying of Edward by Leonora and Nancy in
much the same terms (239). And Dowell, identifying with Edward,
refers to his own pain: 'I have rushed through all Provence—and all
Provence no longer matters. It is no longer in the olive hills that I shall
find my heaven; because there is only hell . . .' (234). His pronounce-
ment sounds like the lament of a rejected poet like Vidal who went
through hell for his love. The irony is obvious.

Vidal's next failure, 'to redeem the Holy Sepulchre', is at once
reminiscent of Edward's desire to build a chapel in tribute to Leonora
and Dowell's failure not only to consummate his marriage with
Florence but also his failure to marry Nancy. He leaves for America 'to
get back into contact with life', to do something masculine but,
thinking of his relationship with Nancy, he says: 'She had frequently
told me that she had no vocation; it just simply wasn't there—the desire
to become a nun. Well, I guess that I was a sort of convent myself, it
seemed fairly proper that she should make her vows to me' (122).
While Edward's failure was the first in a long series of arguments with
Leonora which ultimately led him on an expedition to find the 'ideal
woman', Dowell's failure to 'redeem the Holy Sepulchre' is his failure
to attain masculinity. His trip to America, like Vidal's trip to the Holy
Land, is involved with 'necrological ostentation' and, stranded in a
world of scheming and 'greed of gain' (153), he is called back into the
midst of a domestic war by Edward.

In this story, too, is a cue to Dowell's sexual identity with Edward in
that he, like La Louve's husband is enamoured with Edward's disguise,
his 'wolf-skins', and tries, to a great extent, to dignify Edward's failures
with women. He is demanding, as it were, 'the courtesy due great poets'.
This separation and interchange of identity is a preparation for Dowell's
overt statement later in the novel but the story, in its context as 'culture',
is part of the structural basis for the animal imagery.

In the same context of 'culture' (16) is Dowell's memory of the cows
and his extended simile in which Florence and Leonora are dogs.
Dowell, trying to explain the difference between Florence and Leonora
in matters of culture, uses this comparison:

Have you ever seen a retriever dashing in play after a greyhound? You see
the two running over a green field, almost side by side, and suddenly the
retriever makes a friendly snap at the other. And the greyhound simply

isn't there. You haven't observed it quicken its speed or strain a limb; but there it is, just two yards in front of the retriever's outstretched muzzle. So it was with Florence and Leonora in matters of culture. (41)

To Dowell, they are two breeds of the same species, in friendly competition. Leonora wins. However, Florence's 'friendly snap' is an effort to discover Leonora's reaction to the educating of Edward, but Leonora is already way ahead, knowing what Florence is up to. It is ironic that Dowell, just previous to this analogy, had said that Leonora somehow gave 'the impression of really knowing what poor Florence gave the impression of having only picked up' (40). Florence, as retriever, is picking up more than Dowell is aware of as he 'steers' her toward culture. Leonora is aware of what Florence is trying to pick up and, as Dowell says, 'It was almost something physical' (41).

Juxtaposed to this simile is Dowell's remembered recreation of 'the war of the cows'. In this description he unknowingly relates what will be the outcome of this game of 'culture'. Why is it that the only two laughable events for Dowell, this memory and the Vidal story, are the ones which are latently the most violent, the most revealing?

> Why, I remember on that afternoon I saw a brown cow hitch its horns under the stomach of a black and white animal and the black and white one was thrown right into the middle of a narrow stream. I burst out laughing. But Florence was imparting information so hard and Leonora was listening so intently that no one noticed me. As for me, I was pleased to be off duty; I was pleased to think that Florence for the moment was indubitably out of mischief. . . . I was so relieved to be off duty, because she couldn't possibly be doing anything to excite herself . . . that the incident of the cow was a real joy to me. (42)

In the same context of Florence's weakness and the need to keep her away from exciting topics, Dowell speaks of the Vidal story:

> That is what makes me think of that fellow Peire Vidal. Because, of course, his story is culture and I had to head her towards culture and at the same time it's so funny and she hadn't got to laugh, and it's so full of love and she wasn't to think of love. (16)

Somehow, unconsciously, Dowell connects the ferocious dominance of La Louve and the aggressive overthrow of the black and white cow with the cultural competition between Florence and Leonora for the ownership of Edward. Even when the animals are female, the cows,

Dowell sees them as masculine, in roles of the 'stronger'. The cows, like Florence and Leonora, are seen in this light by Dowell. This overthrow of the cow is re-enacted in the 'protest scene' as Florence takes over Edward's reins from Leonora. Florence is, in effect, overthrowing the present status-quo and with it, Leonora's reign, as she launches her 'protest'. She is 'cutting out and carrying off' her prize right from under the watchful gaze of Leonora.⁹ And this 'cutting out and carrying off' as in polo or in a herd of cattle, becomes the metaphor for the woman as aggressor in cases of adultery. Dowell originally used this metaphor for the way in which Edward operated but as Edward gradually loses the ability to take a male role, especially in his affair with Nancy, Dowell attributes this role to women.

The nature of Dowell's animal imagery, then, as it relates to adultery, is found in an ironic context of 'cultural education' for the male in which the woman, the active guide into adultery, assumes the role of aggressor and fights for control of another woman's husband. Here too, Dowell attributes the male role to the female in that he, as deceived husband, as cuckold, sees instead, the cows, the women, as having horns. In their context as male, Dowell attributes the possession of male genitals and the actions of cuckoldry to the women. This unconscious transference of the male role to the woman, in terms of genital function and cuckoldry, is reinforced in a later chapter in which Dowell sees Leonora as the deceived husband.

The theme of disguise and transference structured in the animal imagery of Part I recurs in Part II in the context of Dowell's memory of his courtship and marriage to Florence. During their courtship, which the Misses Hurlbird oppose, Dowell describes himself as 'a chicken that is determined to get across the road in front of an automobile' (78). In this way he is trying to point out his obstinacy in seeing Florence in spite of opposition, but the image conveys quite a different picture. He implies, through dog imagery, that he was something of a bloodhound as he 'tracked out' Florence (82). Finally, after their marriage, Dowell says that they spent their honeymoon sitting in the woods 'listening to a mocking-bird imitate an old tom-cat' (86). Although Dowell implies that it is he who is imitating the tom-cat ('So I guess Florence had not found getting married to me a very stimulating process' [86]), actually it is Florence, the mock-bird (Hurlbird), who will, by imitating a heart patient, play the tom-cat. Seeing Dowell's restraint and inaction, she will take the aggressive sexual role. She is mocking his passivity by feigning a 'heart' condition so severe that she is unable to bear the passionate outbursts of a newly married husband. Dowell does not apprehend her disguise, her imitation, nor the fact that the mock-bird is really a tom-cat. However, Dowell, too, is a mocking-bird in that he is the female or wife in his marriage; he is the egg-bearer who carries a 'thin-shelled pullet's egg' from Africa to Hoboken. Seeing Florence as a chicken's egg and himself as chicken (78), Dowell makes a symbol of his sacrifice to the potential, unborn sexuality of his marriage. Dowell's carrying of this egg is symbolic of his female role, 'the aspiration that all American women should one day be sexless' (86) but it also symbolizes the mockery of the continually potential, continually unfertilized egg which will never hatch. As his lack of virility is seen in female terms so is his role of cuckold. It is Jimmy, the raven, who has dropped his egg in the nest of another smaller bird, and Dowell, the chicken, is merely feathering a nest around this mockery. However, even the roles of cuckold and cuckold-maker are transferred to Florence and Leonora by Dowell, who says that Leonora 'might then have shared Edward with Florence until the time came for jerking that poor cuckoo out of the nest' (193).[10] The connecting links between these animal images can be traced even in this complex arrangement. Florence, as Jimmy's mistress before her marriage to Dowell, is the egg which the cuckoo-raven, Jimmy, deposits in the nest of a smaller bird. The smaller bird, Dowell, makes a home for this egg thinking it to be his own, or the pullet's egg laid by the chicken. Florence is, thus, the pullet's egg which Dowell carefully nurses and carries. In the group of Florence, Leonora, Dowell and Edward, Dowell sees Edward as the wife, the nest. He sees Leonora as the cuckold and Florence as the deceptive cuckoo. In both cases Dowell assumes a passive role of waiting, nursing whatever egg is dropped in his nest.

Dowell, consciously, sees his relation to the pullet's egg in yet another light. He sees the egg as the symbol of his identity as an athlete, a sportsman like Edward.

> Why, it was as if I had been given a thin-shelled pullet's egg to carry on my palm from Equatorial Africa to Hoboken. Yes, she became for me, as it were, the subject of a bet—the trophy of an athlete's achievement, a parsley crown that is the symbol of his chastity, his soberness, his abstentions, and of his inflexible will. (91–2)

Florence's value as a wife, in Dowell's mind, was extrinsic and symbolic for she had, he says, no intrinsic value for him at all (92). He raises his condition of married celibacy to the level of nobility, to a level on which he is like Edward who, Dowell says, was like 'a painstaking guardian', who appeared the very soul of chastity (11), and who, although Dowell consciously paints him as a 'raging stallion', is seen as the prey of a wife who is the more ferocious soldier of the two. Through his animal imagery we see that Dowell unconsciously pictures Edward as the prey who can, at times, provide a rather convincing imitation of the predator. Dowell, disguising the true condition, tries to ennoble his role as nurse while ennobling the suffering Edward. This idea of the prey imitating the predator, like the bird imitating the cat, is the reverse side of the imagery of role transference or the masculine pretence of virility. In its working out it is Leonora who is the fierce cat and Edward who is the pigeon (130, 178). As the rider, predator, and finally, the ravager, Leonora, although she has control of Edward, is able to disguise her dominance by making him seem like a tin soldier. Dowell seems to imply that Leonora willingly set Edward up as a well-dressed decoy, sexually as well as financially (168), saying that 'Leonora imagined the cheerful device of letting him see the accounts of his estate' (169), but, in reality, Edward was only an imitation husband.

Dowell, whose position even as potential male is mocked and undercut by Florence, is still weakly able to imitate virility, as her 'husband', and by ennobling his role of trained poodle to symbolic significance. Overtly, Dowell poses as male by his juggling of identity with Edward, the good soldier, but covertly, his desire for identity is so strong that, unconsciously, through his animal imagery, he not only equates himself with Edward as decoy, as imitation male, but also he reduces Edward to a passive animal preyed upon by aggressive females. If, as Dowell says, Leonora was pimping for Edward, then Edward was the prostitute and, even in this, Dowell seeks a diluted identity; he thinks that he, too, had been made the commodity which his wife used for her own devices. In all ways Dowell identifies with Edward; as sportsman (91-2), for, although Florence is the trophy, they share her; as dog-nurse (63, 166), in fashion (25-6), in mutual conventions (37), in mental appearance (11-12), as lover (114-15), and finally, as Edward himself, the owner of Branshaw and celibate lover of Nancy (253).

In a series of images we see Edward, beginning as the 'raging stallion', successively reduced to become merely the unconscious pigeon, the decoy, the prey, the tin soldier and imitation-landowner and, finally, the dumb, beaten brute lashed and torn by she-wolves. It is at this point in Edward's dog-like passivity that Dowell can make an overt statement, not of identity, but of complete assimilation with him. Dowell's identity seems to be part of an ambivalently emotional and vicariously sexual participation in Edward's life which was implied as early as the Vidal story (16–17) in which Dowell unconsciously split the two aspects of Edward's nature (poet-soldier), assumed the role of substitute singer (jongleur) and, by the time he had completed his narrative it was impossible for him to tell the singer from the song.

Dowell's ambivalence and his division of Edward's personality is, at once, the conscious and unconscious rendering of his narrative function. Dowell is aware of a duality in himself when he says, 'I suppose that my inner soul—my dual personality—had realized' (121). Trying to explain his verbalized desire to marry Nancy spoken at the time of Florence's death, he says, 'It is as if one had a dual personality, the one I being entirely unconscious of the other' (103). Dowell, however, isolates the evidence of his duality as an unconsciously verbalized emotion of which he was unaware, but his duality, like Edward's, is part of the game of social and sexual 'shuttlecocks'. In his mental shuffling or juggling of events, in his shifting of male and female roles, in his 'passion' to be a participant rather than a 'trained poodle'—a man who had, after 'twelve years of the repression of his instincts' (120), awakened to find himself not an heroically long-suffering bearer of a wifely burden, ennobled by sacrifice, but still only a trained poodle trapped by the very nature of his conditioned responses—Dowell is trying to hold onto a phantom thread while moving through 'what may be a sort of maze' (183). The back and forth motion of his narrative thread is his unconscious rendering of the unconscious meaning in the game of shuttlecocks because, if he can get the 'birdie' moving fast enough across the net, so fast that the shuttlecock cannot be distinguished from a 'real' bird, then he can not only seem, but be the good soldier. Although aware that he lacks the 'courage', 'virility' and 'physique', he does possess, in the same way Edward possessed, Branshaw and Nancy. Dowell lacked the 'apparent' means to consummate his desires and consciously finds in Edward what he calls 'a larger elder brother who took me out on several excursions and did many dashing things whilst I just watched him robbing the orchards, from a distance' (253-4). This is a seeming affirmation of his vicarious identity with Edward, an aligning of self which he previously described as Edward's basis for seeking women, and his real passion. Dowell, however, makes it the basis for his assimilation of Edward's identity.

> But the real fierceness of desire, the real heat of passion long continued and withering up the soul of a man, is the craving for identity with the woman that he loves. He desires to see with the same eyes ... to hear with the same ears, to lose his identity, to be enveloped. ... We are all so alone, we all so need *from the outside* the assurance of our own worthiness to exist. (114-15. Italics added.)

Dowell has achieved this very identity with Edward; enveloping himself in an unconscious and unthreatening version of Edward, he is assured, from the outside, through his possession of the very object of Edward's desire, and an almost hereditary ownership of his property, as younger brother. The end result of the complete absorption of identity is seen in a way that is below the level of Dowell's consciousness. His 'craving for identity' with Edward is also his desire, in a female role, to 'lose his identity'. This can be made possible only through a narrative recreation in which an unconscious manipulation of images provides a transference of roles and a reduction in character. This substructure is made manifest by certain cues which Dowell does not connect, but inadvertently reveals as part of his memory process. What reminds him that he has forgotten to tell of Edward's suicide? Dowell learns from Edward that he is 'so desperately in love with Nancy Rufford that [he] is dying of it' (250). The next day the three of them go to the station to see Nancy off and then 'everything went on as if the girl never existed'. This is where Dowell seems to end his narrative of past events and continues with present conditions (252). In this present situation Dowell says that he sits in Edward's gun-room all day, and this is, no doubt, where he is writing. He dines with Nancy and walks beneath 'his' oaks, 'his' clumps of gorse, seeing 'his' tenants tip their hats (254). If it is true that Dowell owns only the shell of Branshaw and nurses only the shell of Nancy, it is also true that Edward, forced to the wall by Leonora, owned only this same shell. Edward had symbolically become an imitation stallion and landowner. He gave his newly invented stirrup to the army (195). He gave his horse to a young boy whose father had been ruined. He gives away his stirrup, his symbolic hold on life as good soldier in a feudal system of warrior-landowner, and next, he gives away his Irish horse, symbolic of his sexuality, his mount, his wife who really husbands him both sexually and financially. Having given up his identity, he merely sits in his gun-room, under a mantelpiece full of remnants of his former identity with spurs, hooves, models of horses, and a picture of a horse (212). It is in this room that Dowell says that Leonora lashes at Edward about Nancy and all his previous affairs. It is in this room that Dowell listens to Edward's confession of love for Nancy as he talks all through the night (249). It is in this room that Dowell ends the writing of his story (254). All that is left of Edward in his identity with the stallion is the immobile, framed picture of a white horse on a brownish background. This is his symbolic reduction to the imitation, the shell, and it is now Dowell's possession. He forgets to tell about the death of Edward Ashburnham because the real death took place sometime before the actual suicide. The telling of it is an afterthought on Dowell's part because he has assumed the role, taken possession; Dowell is Edward, and still alive.

If we follow the cues begun with the Vidal story and follow the progression of the animal imagery in relation to character, we see that there is a dual but simultaneous action in that, as the animals used to focus character gradually become more pejorative in connotation, showing a deterioration of Edward and Leonora, so Dowell, in the unconscious narrative process, comes to a closer and closer identity with Edward and a greater and greater hatred of Leonora. When these two lines of action join, Dowell is Edward and Leonora is merely a rabbit-like female. As horsewoman, Leonora was in a relationship of seeming compromise with her mount. When rider becomes predator, all contact is destroyed and Edward's 'preliminary canters', or affairs, are only graceful steps before the final headlong gallop to death (116). In short, when Leonora was the rider, Edward's affairs are controlled canters, but when she becomes predator and hungry pursuer, his canters become gallops. No longer reined in, Edward's race begins and the more slack Leonora allows him, the more furious are her lashings. She begins by reining but ends by lashing and flaying.

Dowell's reaction to Leonora and her 'rabbit-like' husband, Rodney Bayham, may be explained as the unimportant aspect of what he calls 'the true passion', the physical consummation that is taken for granted and is of a lower order than Dowell's own assimilation of Edward (114–15).

Dowell's rendering of the 'saddest story' becomes, through the vehicle of a substructure of animal imagery, the story of a poodle who thought he became a stallion. Through the themes of disguise, identity and the transference of male and female roles, the movement of the animal imagery, as it illuminates character and action, takes a subterranean course parallel to the surface course, ending in a sudden artesian fountain at the point of juncture in which both Dowell and Edward are one. As Edward could talk to Dowell since he 'appeared to be a woman or solicitor', so Dowell can become Edward by transferring male and female roles.[11]

It has been said that Dowell and Edward are comic and tragic counterparts, that Dowell would like to be Edward, and that Dowell speaks in two voices, the one dogmatic, the other bewildered. While such a relationship and duality exist, it is closer to the point to say that in the implicit meaning of the pattern of animal imagery we find Dowell's second voice, and the means by which he actually becomes Edward. Dowell, unconsciously, is a wife in sentiment and in his commitment to passivity, but Edward was manipulated toward this role. His identity with Edward is, at once, both masculine and feminine for, while he is still a nurse, he is nurse and heir to the good soldier's fortune.

SOURCE: *Critique*, IX (1966).

NOTES

1. See Todd K. Bender, 'The Sad Tale of Dowell', *Criticism* (Fall 1962), p. 361ff; James Hafley, 'The Moral Structure of *The Good Soldier*', *Modern Fiction Studies* (Summer 1959); Eliot P. Gose, 'The Strange Irregular Rhythm', *PMLA*, LXII (June 1957); Robert J. Andreach, 'The Quest for Permanence and Stability', *Tennessee Studies in Literature* (1965).

2. Samuel Hynes, 'The Epistemology of *The Good Soldier*', see above, pp. 97–105. James Trammell Cox, 'Ford's Passion for Provence', *English Literary History*, XXVIII (Dec. 1961).

3. See Hynes, p. 100 above for a discussion of these indirect means and his choice of the narrator's development via *The Great Gatsby*.

4. Vintage edition, New York, 1951.

5. John Meixner, *Ford Madox Ford's Novels* (Minneapolis, 1962) pp. 150–89, especially pp. 174–81.

6. See Richard Cassell, *Ford Madox Ford* (Baltimore, 1961) pp. 191–201. For the categories of imagery see pp. 191–2.

7. Shakespeare, *Much Ado About Nothing* (I i 48–9) contains the following repartee: '*Messenger*: And [he is] a Good Soldier too, lady. *Beatrice*: And a Good Soldier to a lady.' The meaning, in the first speech, is the heroic and courteous behavior of the soldier while, in the second, Beatrice is referring to the soldier's sexual prowess and his ability as a 'rider'. Since these two meanings are both parts of Edward's identity as a Good Soldier, ironically intended or not, it seems that this is a likely contender for the source of Ford's revised title, in spite of the fact that he seems to have found it on the spur of the moment. The irony of this, as Ford says (xxii), is 'a two-edged sword'.

8. Hynes, 'Epistemology', see above, pp. 97–105.

9. For these references to 'cutting out and carrying off' see pp. 29–30, 71, 116, 144. The structural basis is in Edward's cutting out and carrying off the point in polo. Then, the contexts for this metaphor become sexual: as Edward's method with women, as Florence's taking of Edward, and as the general state of female reactions to husbands who seem to be abused by their wives.

10. *Cuckoo's nest* is a slang term for the female genitals. *Horns* can refer both to the male genitals and to the horns of a cuckold. *Horned Herd* refers to the general category of cuckolds. *Horning* is adulterous intercourse. Cuckoo: 'the cuckoo then on every tree mocks the married man' (*Love's Labour's Lost*, v ii); a bird which lays its eggs in the nest of smaller birds (the 'cuckold' does not, rather he cares for the false eggs). See Eric Partridge, *Shakespeare's Bawdy* (New York, 1960) pp. 97, 129–30. Dowell calls Florence the cuckoo, the maker of a cuckold, or the male who, by adulterous intercourse with the cuckold's wife, may leave his egg in the nest of another; he may leave the deceived husband a false egg (child) to take care of and the husband will think it to be his own. In this relation Leonora is the cuckold, the betrayed husband who discovers a 'mock-bird' in the nest. Edward, the wife, is the 'nest' (female genitals) out of which Florence, the male lover and cuckold-maker, would be jerked by the irate 'husband'. In this transference of male and female roles, the relationship of Dowell as egg-carrier becomes more clearly symbolic, for he, in this female role, identifies Edward as the wife of Leonora, thus seeing Edward as the passive partner. Dowell seems to be drawing Edward into his own disguise. The double reference of 'horns', as those of the cuckold and also of the male doing the 'horning', illuminates Dowell's description of his memory of the cows. Florence is horning Leonora by adulterous intercourse (Florence as lover) and Leonora, the overthrown, wears the horns of the deceived husband. We see this supplanting in the 'protest' scene. Thus, Florence in a male role is the aggressive, virile lover and Leonora is the cuckold. The horn-made and the horn-maker are both seen as cows. The idea of 'horns' for the cuckold, and horn representing the erect male organ, comes from the myth in which Jove transformed himself into a horned bull for amorous purposes. This myth of *Europe and Jove* shows the origin of the Cretan King Minos and Pasiphae, his wife, who conceived the minotaur by coupling with a white bull. In disgrace, Minos had a huge maze, or labyrinth, built in which he lived and hid Pasiphae and the minotaur at the heart of it. There is a resemblance between this myth and Dowell's process of mentation as he says: 'I have, I am aware, told this story in a very rambling way so that it may be difficult for anyone to find his path through what may be a sort of maze' (183). His intellectual and emotional method of narration is the maze and his condition at the end of the novel is that of Minos, a judge in Hades who tries the most difficult cases. There are many other parallels between this myth and the novel. See Robert Graves, *The Greek Myths*. Dowell's transference of male and female roles makes his overt identification with Edward possible, in terms of their female identity and, also, joins with the theme of disguise in that the birds which can disguise their songs or imitate the songs of other birds are the cuckoo, the mocking-

bird and the raven. Dowell, Florence and Jimmy, and Edward, through the vehicle of Dowell's animal imagery, all become, in some way, mock-birds, or assume a disguise for the purposes of deception. Dowell assumes the wife, Florence is the mock-bird, the hurl-bird who, in her disguise as a heart patient, not only mocks Dowell but hurls Leonora into midstream. Jimmy, the raven, supplants or overthrows Dowell and leaves him with a pullet's egg to nurse, thus Dowell is never an active male. The sexual mocking-bird can imitate or disguise itself at will.

11. The idea of role transference is supported by the connotations of the characters' names. We see that the women's names all carry the connotation of action, of some violent act or quality (*Ruf-ford*; *Hurl*-bird; *Powys*—power, prowess), while the men's names imply an ending action (*Ash-burn*-ham) or an ironic sexual pun (Do-well). On the female side there are the connotations of the rough, the wild and the animal, but the male names are connected with the domestic, the hearth. For another version of the meaning of Dowell's name see Neil D. Isaacs, 'The Narrator of *The Good Soldier*', *English Literature in Transition*, VI (1963).

WILLIAM CARLOS WILLIAMS

Parade's End (1951)

EVERY time we approach a period of transition someone cries out: This is the last! the last of Christianity, of the publishing business, freedom for the author, the individual! Thus we have been assured that in this novel, *Parade's End*, we have a portrait of the last Tory. But what in God's name would Ford Madox Ford be doing writing the tale of the last Tory? He'd far rather have tied it into black knots.

In a perfectly appointed railway carriage, two young men of the British public official class, close friends, are talking quietly together. Back of their minds stands Great Groby House, the Tietjens' family seat, in Yorkshire, the north of England—its people, neighbors, and those associated with them just prior to the beginning of the First World War. It was a noteworthy transition period. It would be idle of me, an American, to try to recreate so highly flavored an atmosphere as that represented in this railway carriage. One of the speakers is Christopher Tietjens, younger son to Groby's ancestral proprietor; he is a blond hulk of a man, a sharp contrast to his companion, Macmaster, dark-haired and with a black pointed beard, a smallish Scotsman for whom the Tietjens family has provided a little money to get him through Cambridge and establish him in Town.

Sylvia, young Christopher's beautiful wife, has four months previously gone off to the Continent with a lover. She has sickened of him and wants to be taken back. The two men on the train, thoroughly well bred and completely British, are discussing the circumstance and its probable outcome—Christopher, defending his wife, has consented to let her do as she pleases. There begins now to unravel (you might almost say it is Christopher's ungainly bulk itself that is unraveling) as intimate, full, and complex a tale as you will find under the official veneer of our day.

Four books, *Some Do Not* ..., *No More Parades*, *A Man Could*

F.M.F.—5

Stand Up, and *The Last Post,* have been for the first time offered in one volume as Ford had wished it. The title, *Parade's End,* is his own choosing. Together they constitute the English prose masterpiece of their time. But Ford's writings have never been popular, as popular, let's say, as the writings of Proust have been popular. Yet they are written in a style that must be the envy of every thinking man. The pleasure in them is infinite.

When I first read the books I began, by chance, with *No More Parades*; as the story ran the First World War was in full swing, the dirt, the deafening clatter, the killing. So it was a little hard for me to retreat to *Some Do Not,* which deals with the social approaches to that holocaust. At once, in the first scenes of this first book the conviction is overwhelming that we are dealing with a major talent. We are plunged into the high ritual of a breakfast in the Duchemin drawing room—all the fine manners of an established culture. There's very little in English to surpass that, leading as it does to the appearance of the mad cleric himself, who for the most part lies secretly closeted in his own home. Beside this we have the relationship of the man's tortured wife with Tietjens' friend Macmaster; the first full look at Valentine Wannop and of Tietjens himself before he appears in khaki—the whole rotten elegance of the business; Sylvia, at her best, and the old lady's 'You are so beautiful, my dear, you must be good.' Then it shifts to Christopher and the girl, Valentine, in the fog, linking the land, disappointment, the yearning for fulfillment and—the ten-foot-deep fog itself covering everything but the stars of a brilliant sky overhead; we see Christopher in the carriage holding the reins, Valentine leaping down to find a road sign and disappearing from his view. Only the horse's head, as he tosses it, reappears to Christopher from time to time as the man sits there alone. Following that is the restraint and hatred in the scene between husband and wife, Christopher and Sylvia. He at table in uniform, she standing behind him, bored. Casually she flings the contents of her plate at the back of his neck, glad she hadn't actually hit him—but the oil from the dressing dribbled down on his insignia. He didn't even turn. It is their farewell as he is about to leave for the front.

This is the first of the four books. The war intervenes. *No More Parades.* The war ends. Tietjens is invalided home, his mind half gone. Valentine lives for him and he recovers. Mark, the present heir to

Groby, the Correct Man, represents the family and England as a family. Living with his French mistress he suffers a cerebral hemorrhage and lies, during all of *The Last Post*, in a sort of summerhouse, where with his last breath, and as he holds the pregnant Valentine by the hand, the saga comes to an end.

Sylvia, through all the books, in her determination to destroy her husband, does everything a woman can, short of shooting him, to accomplish her wish. From start to finish she does not falter.

This is where an analysis should begin: for some, who have written critically of *Parade's End*, find Sylvia's extreme hatred of her husband, her inexorable, even doctrinaire hatred, unreal. I think they are wrong. All love between these two or the possibility for it was spent before the story began when Christopher lay with his wife-to-be, unknowing, in another railway carriage, immediately after her seduction by another man. It made an impossible situation. From that moment all that was left for them was love's autopsy, an autopsy and an awakening—an awakening to a new *form* of love, the first liberation from his accepted Toryism. Sylvia was done. Valentine up! A new love had already begun to shimmer above the fog before his intelligence, a new love with which the past was perhaps identical, or had been identical, but in other terms. Sylvia suffers also, while a leisurely torment drives her to desperation. It is the very slowness of her torment, reflected in the minutiae, the passionate dedication, the last agonized twist of Ford's style, that makes the story move.

In his very perception and love for the well observed detail lies Ford's narrative strength, the down-upon-it affection for the thing itself in which he is identical with Tietjens, his prototype. In spite of all changes, in that, at least, the Tory carries over: concern for the care of the fields, the horses, whatever it may be; the landed proprietor must be able to advise his subordinates who depend on him, he is responsible for them also. That at least was Tietjens, that too was Ford.

When you take those qualities of a man over into the new conditions, the Tory conditions that Tietjens paradoxically loved, the whole picture must be altered—and a confusion, a tragic confusion, results, needing to be righted; it is an imperative that becomes a moral duty as well as a duty to letters.

Ford, like Tietjens, paid attention to these things. I'll not forget when he came to visit me in Rutherford, a town lying in the narrow sun-baked strip of good soil, land which the Dutch farmers cultivated so well in the old days, between the low Watchung Range and the swampy land of the Hackensack Meadows. It is one of the best tilled, you might almost say currycombed, bits of the Garden State as New Jersey is still called. Old Ford, for he was old by that time, was interested. He asked me to take him out to see the truck farms. We spent the afternoon at it, a blistering July day when the sprinkler system was turned on in many of the fields, straight back into the country, about three or four miles, to the farm of Derrick Johnson, who personally showed us around. I was more interested in the sandpipers running through the tilled rows— birds which I hadn't seen up to then other than running on the wet sand of beaches as the water washed up and retreated, uncovering minute food. But on the farm they were nesting, here their eggs were laid and hatched in the heat between the beet rows on the bare ground. But Ford, who was looking around, questioned the farmer closely about the cultivation of the lettuce, carrots, dandelion, leeks, peppers, tomatoes, and radishes which he was raising. It was all part of his understanding of the particular—and of what should properly occupy and compel a man's mind. He might have been Tietjens.

So far I have spoken in the main of Christopher and Sylvia, their relationship, their positions and their marriage. But there are other characters as important in the argument as they. Mark, Christopher's elder brother, the one man whom Sylvia has never been able to impress, should be put down as the first of these—as Ford, I think, recognizes, when he makes him the key figure of the entire last book, *The Last Post*. Mark, the perfectly cultured gentleman. Professor Wannop, old friend of the family, a studious recluse who has brought up his daughter, Valentine, in his own simple and profound ways, is gone. And there is, of course, Valentine herself, though she appears, generally speaking, little. She fills, however, a dominant place. *A Man Could Stand Up* is her book. General Campion, official England, is another to be named. He will carry off the girl, old as he is, at the close. At every turn he appears, often as Sylvia's instrument to thwart Christopher, triumphant officialdom.

But greater than he, Tietjens, are the men in the trenches, his special responsibilities, over whom he pains, a bumbling mother, exhausting himself to the point of mental and physical collapse.

Few could be in the position which Ford himself occupied in English society to know these people. His British are British in a way the American, Henry James, never grasped. They fairly smell of it. The true test is his affection for them, top to bottom, a moral, not a literary attribute, his love of them, his wanting to be their Moses, to lead them out of captivity to their rigid aristocratic ideals—to the ideals of a new aristocracy. Ford like Tietjens was married to them and like Sylvia they were determined to destroy him for it. Even when he could help them, as Tietjens helped Macmaster, Ford got kicked for it and was thrown out of the paradise of their dying ideas—as much by D. H. Lawrence on one side, the coal miner's son, as by the others. He helped Lawrence but Lawrence soon backed out. And still no one grasps the significance of Tietjens' unending mildness, torn between the two forces—no one, really, but Valentine and Mark in the last words.

Sylvia's bitter and unrelenting hatred for Tietjens, her husband, is the dun mountain under the sunrise, the earth itself of the old diabolism. We sense, again and again, more than is stated, two opposing forces. Not who but *what* is Sylvia? (I wonder if Ford with his love of the Elizabethan lyric didn't have that in mind when he named her.)

At the start her husband has, just too late for him, found out her secret; and feeling a responsibility, almost a pity for her, has assumed a superior moral position which she cannot surmount or remove. She had been rudely seduced, and on the immediate rebound, you might almost say with the same gesture, married Tietjens in self defen.e. She cannot even assure her husband that the child is his own. She cannot be humble without denying all her class prerogatives. Christopher's mere existence is an insult to her. But to have him pity her is hellish torment. She is forced by everything that is holy to make him a cuckold, again and again. For England itself in her has been attacked. But Valentine can pick up her young heels, as she did at the golf course, and leap a ditch, a thing impossible for Sylvia unless she change her clothes, retrain her muscles and unbend.

But there is a deeper reason than that—and a still more paradoxical—in that Tietjens forced her to do good; that as his wife she serves best when she most hates him. The more she lies the better she serves. This is truly comic. And here a further complexity enters. Let me put it this way: if there is one thing I cannot accede to in a commonality of

aspiration, it is the loss of the personal and the magnificent . . . the mind
that cannot contain itself short of that which makes for great shows.
Not wealth alone but a wealth that enriches the imagination. Such a
woman is Sylvia, representing the contemporary emblazonments of
medieval and princely retinue. How can we take over our *Kultur*, a
trait of aristocracy, without a Sylvia, in short as Tietjens desired her?
What is our drabness beside the magnificence of a Sistine Chapel, a
gold salt cellar by Cellini, a Taj, a great wall of China, a Chartres? The
mind is the thing not the cut stone but the stone itself. The words of a
Lear. The sentences of *Some Do Not* themselves that are not likely for
this to be banished from our thoughts.

Ford gave the woman, Sylvia, life; let her exercise her full range of
feeling, vicious as it might be, her full armament of woman. Let her be
what she *is*. Would Tietjens divorce her? When there is reason yes,
but so long as she is truthfully what she is and is fulfilling what she is
manifestly *made* to be, he has nothing but respect for her. Ford uses her
to make a meaning. She will not wobble or fail. It is not his business.
This is a way of looking at the word.

Ford's philosophy in these novels is all of a piece, character and
writing. The word keeps the same form as the characters' deeds or the
writer's concept of them. Sylvia is the dead past in all its affecting
glamor. Tietjens is in love the while with a woman of a different order,
of no landed distinction, really a displaced person seeking replacement.
Valentine Wannop is the reattachment of the word to the object—it
is obligatory that the protagonist (Tietjens) should fall in love with her,
she is Persephone, the rebirth, the reassertion—from which we today
are at a nadir, the lowest ebb.

Sylvia is the lie, boldfaced, the big crude lie, the denial . . . that is now
having its moment. The opponent not of *le mot juste* against which the
French have today been rebelling, but something of much broader
implications; so it must be added that if our position in the world, the
democratic position, is difficult, and we must acknowledge that it is
difficult, the Russian position, the negative position, the lying position,
that is, the Communist position is still more difficult. All that is implied
in Ford's writing.

To use the enormous weapon of the written word, to speak accurately that is (in contradiction to the big crude lie) is what Ford is building
here. For Ford's novels are written with a convinced idea of respect for

the meaning of the words—and what a magnificent use they are put to in his hands! whereas the other position is not conceivable except as disrespect for the word's meaning. He speaks of this specifically in *No More Parades*—that no British officer can read and understand a simple statement unless it be stereotype . . . disrespect for the word and that, succinctly put, spells disaster.

Parenthetically, we shall have to go through some disastrous passages, make no mistake about that, but sooner or later we shall start uphill to our salvation. There is no other way. For in the end we must stand upon one thing and that only, respect for the word, and that is the one thing our enemies do not have. Therefore rejoice, says Ford, we have won our position and will hold it. But not yet—except in microcosm (a mere novel you might say). For we are sadly at a loss except in the reaches of our best minds to which Ford's mind is a prototype.

At the end Tietjens sees everything upon which his past has been built tossed aside. His brother has died, the inheritance is vanished, scattered, in one sense wasted. He sees all this with perfect equanimity —Great Groby Tree is down, the old curse achieved through his first wife's beneficent malevolence, a malevolence which he perfectly excuses. He is stripped to the rock of belief. But he is not really humili-ated since he has kept his moral integrity through it all. In fact it is that which has brought him to destruction. All that by his up-bringing and conviction he has believed is the best of England, save for Valentine, is done. But those who think that that is the end of him miss the whole point of the story, they forget the Phoenix symbol, the destruction by fire to immediate rebirth. Mark dead, Christopher, his younger brother, has got Valentine with child.

This is not the 'last Tory' but the first in the new enlightenment of the Englishman—at his best, or the most typical Englishman. The sort of English that fought for and won Magna Carta, having undergone successive mutations through the ages, has reappeared in another form. And this we may say, I think, is the story of these changes, this decline and the beginning of the next phase. Thus it is not the facile legend, 'the Last Tory', can describe that of which Ford is speaking, except in a secondary sense, but the tragic emergence of the first Tory of the new dispensation—as Christopher Tietjens and not without international implications. *Transition* was the biggest word of the quarter century with which the story deals, though its roots, like those of Groby Great

Tree, lie in a soil untouched by the modern era. *Parade's End* then is for me a tremendous and favorable study of the transition of England's most worthy type, in Ford's view and affections, to the new man and what happens to him. The sheer writing can take care of itself.

SOURCE: W. C. Williams, *Selected Essays* (1954).

MARLENE GRIFFITH

A Double Reading of
Parade's End (1963)

ONE of the problems which has engulfed twentieth century fiction is the relation between external and internal reality. Nineteenth century novels teemed with a bustling social reality. Becky Sharp calls its bluff and declares her challenge when she throws Johnson's dictionary out the carriage window. She does not analyze motives or doubt self; she acts against a stable world which is excluding her. *David Copperfield* may be a form of the *Bildungsroman*, but it primarily concerns itself with telling us what has happened to this young man without exploring the whys, and we know him as we know the boy next door. The story is rich in incident, rich in people: we are delighted that Barkis is willin'; we hate Murdstone with a clean and unambiguous hatred. Such novels probe hypocrisies, criticize social evils, and create full worlds for our enjoyment and instruction by building on a shared system of values and relying on a common language.

Preceded by Darwin, Freud, and Virginia Woolf's 1910, the shock of the First World War decisively endstops the Victorian age and illuminates the break-up of old orientations. We suddenly have new concepts of time and of consciousness, which relocate the center of reality within the individual, away from the social world. Established values are undercut; the novelist must rethink the process of selection, and traditional techniques and conventions become useless. What *is* important? Once the core of reality is set within the individual, separated from others by a separate consciousness and with no unifying bridge, we find that more is unique than shared; everything is relative in terms of individual perception so that even society becomes unreal and communication distorted. Loneliness becomes the predominant theme, counteracted by an enormous need to break through and communicate on a meaningful and significant level.[1] We are led to the interior monologue—a new method to touch an elusive new reality—which, however, does not prove wholly satisfactory as an end in itself since there is more to reality than the circumscribed inner world of the individual consciousness.

At this point, in the novel at least, the skin of external reality was shed in the attempt to come to grips with internal reality. Rarely did the two coexist successfully. If we take some of Dickens as an extreme example of the one school, we may perhaps take Virginia Woolf as an extreme example of the other. Few have been able to come to grips with both. Isabel Archer moves in a closed social circle among expatriates and aristocrats. Heyst fights his demons on a South Seas island. Most writers focus on individuals at the expense of society or on society at the expense of individuals, or, at best, put their characters on the periphery of either the one or the other. Few have been able to embrace both social reality and personal sensibility, yet one needs the other to give it meaning.

One of the few writers who has, to my mind, been successful in embracing both is Ford Madox Ford. The book: *Parade's End.* Looking at these four volumes as one unit, I think it is possible to discern two interrelated but nevertheless separate patterns, the world of social experience (external reality) and the world of personal sensibility (internal reality), and to show that these patterns culminate in two distinct climaxes.

Ford's comment on what I choose to call external reality can best be traced if we see this book as centering on a man with traditional virtues who slowly discards the fraudulent and embraces the real: who moves from a passive existence in a social framework to an active existence in a highly individual framework, and in so doing redefines not only his virtues but also his world. Through Tietjens, Ford is able to probe the world around him; he presents a novel of social decay, and in such a reading the climax falls on the felling of the Groby Great Tree in *The Last Post*, the book's final volume.

We begin in *Some Do Not* with a panoramic world, centered, to be sure, upon Christopher Tietjens, but Tietjens against society; as we proceed, the scope narrows until the world with which he interacts has been reduced to three or four people. Although Ford's over-all style is unmistakable—the time shift and interior monologue, the outlining then the filling in, so that the volumes not only continue but also reinforce one another—it should be noted that as the area of significance shifts, technique changes. In the beginning Ford leans heavily on third-person narrative, which can establish and depict a social world; in the end he restricts himself almost entirely to the interior monologue and gains in depth what he loses in breadth.

If a world is to crumble, we must know what that world is, and if people are to find or lose their way in this world, we must know who these people are. The key figure, Christopher Tietjens, youngest son of the Groby Tietjens, is 'very big, in a fair, untidy, Yorkshire way',[2] a good classicist, a brilliant mathematician who in his spare time occupies himself by 'tabulating from memory the errors in the *Encyclopaedia Brittannica*' (p. 10), lumbering, aloof, non-competitive, and lacking in self-pity, a man who is 'so formal that he can't do without all the conventions there are and so truthful he can't use half of them' (p. 32). Tietjens is the last Tory. He has inner order; he has stability.

Around Tietjens, Ford erects his world. There is Sylvia, his wife, beautiful, Catholic and bored, who married Christopher when she feared herself pregnant by another man, and has hated and loved him since. She is dedicated to and adept at tormenting him if for no other reason than to break down his Jehovah-like treatment of her and evoke, for once, a human response. There is Valentine Wannop, born in the old tradition but living in the new. Forced into domestic service after her father's death, she is the best Latinist in England, a social radical, a suffragette, young, active, alive, and feeling. There is her mother who has 'written the only novel worth reading since the eighteenth century' (p. 73). There is Macmaster who today might be the angry young man but in Ford's world was the outsider wanting to become part of a tradition to which he did not belong. Tietjens' erstwhile school friend, an amateur literary critic, Macmaster eventually receives a knighthood by semi-fraudulent means and later establishes a literary salon. There is the Reverend Mr Duchemin, former student of Ruskin, with scato-logical weaknesses. There is his wife:widow, a Pre-Raphaelite beauty, circumspect and right, who becomes, first, Macmaster's mistress and then his wife. There is General Campion, Tietjens' godfather and an admirer of Sylvia. There is Mark, Tietjens' half-brother, taciturn, shrewd, and ordered. There is a multiplicity of social types.

The book begins in a railway carriage, and the first sentence could belong to any number of standard nineteenth-century novels: 'The two young men—they were of the English public official class—sat in the perfectly appointed railway carriage.' This railway carriage leads us into the Edwardian world of country weekends, golf courses, clubs, bachelor quarters, and Whitehall offices, but it is a world beginning to shake. The golf course is invaded by suffragettes; the country breakfast is shattered by Duchemin's indecencies; city men with oily hair invade private clubs and discuss their domestic circumstances in a loud voice, and gentlemen can no longer trust each other. Tietjens' personal code is based upon the ability to trust one's equals, a trust which is violated by Sylvia's slanderous but successful intrigues. By the end of the volume Christopher has cut himself off from Groby, from his club, and has been cut by the social world in which he moves.

What is important is that in *Some Do Not* Ford builds a complex and panoramic world around his main character. In *No More Parades*, the second volume, he shifts backgrounds and narrows the focus of his lens. It is now 1914; we are behind the lines in France, where Tietjens is in charge of troop transports. War is the backdrop, and it is a cold, an exhausting, and a worrisome backdrop. Apparent order has given way to chaos, and when Tietjens, suffering from partial amnesia, fears for his mind, he seeks control by asking for fourteen end rhymes and setting himself the task of writing a sonnet in under two minutes and a half. His old world intrudes upon him (the middle part of the book is devoted to Sylvia's intrusion) but Tietjens is nevertheless separated from it, both geographically and spiritually.

After expending a whole volume on two days with Tietjens behind the lines, Ford now telescopes our view still further and, in *A Man Could Stand Up*, shows us Armistice day at home and, in a flashback, a day at the front. He does two things in this volume. First he has to fully detach Tietjens from his world in order to allow him to re-examine it, once and for all to separate appearances from realities, and to allow him to return to it. He does this by showing Tietjens at the front in a war that is muddy, wet, and cold; a waiting war where communications have broken down. Again fearing for his mind, Tietjens this time can draw *only* on himself to maintain his sanity. He does so by recalling the sane seventeenth century, by recalling Anglican sainthood, by recalling George Herbert at Bemerton and the lines '*Sweet day so cool, so calm, so bright, the bridal of the earth and sky!*' (p. 586). At the same time, Ford prepares for Tietjens' return by starting the book on Armistice morning in England with Valentine, and is thus able to end it on Armistice night in England with Valentine and Christopher.

This, then, leads us to *The Last Post*, where we have the final with-drawal and detachment, combined with the final return. We are back in England, this time in a pastoral setting, and Christopher's world has narrowed down to Valentine, Mark, and, on the fringe, Mark's wife.

To recapitulate, the unifying line is as follows: at the center we have Christopher Tietjens, always aloof, but at the beginning moving in a social world in which he does not really fit but in which, as a Tietjens of Groby, he has a place. As we proceed through the four volumes, Ford allows this world to become more and more remote or, depending on our viewpoint, allows Tietjens to become more and more detached from it. The greater the detachment, the more imperative it is for Tietjens to re-evaluate. When detached—and a soldier at the front *is* detached—it is easier to distinguish the important from the unimportant, to distinguish the valid from the invalid, the appearance from the reality, and Ford is telling us that we cannot embrace until we have experienced alienation. After the war, Tietjens is able to rejoin his world physically, but to detach himself from it spiritually. He forsakes the traditional apparatus surrounding him and, hopefully, begins a new tradition from within.

Such a reading lends itself to an allegorial interpretation wherein Tietjens becomes a symbol. In his illuminating article, 'Tietjens and the Tradition',[3] Joseph J. Firebaugh traces an allegory of social decay, pointing out that Tietjens, the last Tory, stands for the traditional virtues and represents the England which is decaying. Sylvia represents the world of appearances—her neurosis is the neurosis of the modern world; Macmasters represents the arriviste who defeats the traditional values by spurious emulation. Both embody symptoms of social decay. Valentine represents the social radical, and it is only when Tietjens: England can actively embrace the social radical and discard the fraud-ulence which has attached itself to traditional virtues that salvation is possible. The future is implied both by the Marxian heir to Groby, Tietjens' legitimate son by Sylvia, and by the illegitimate, as yet unborn child of the Last Tory and the social radical.

Clearly this is a valid reading, and once we begin hunting for allegory we find ourselves amply rewarded. At the end of *Some Do Not*, for example, Tietjens suffers from partial amnesia, and for amnesia we can read withdrawal. As he regains his memory, step by laborious step, he fights for his sanity (order) which he feels threatened by an insane (disordered) world. He wins in this fight, whereas McKechnie, the mad-eyed Latin prize man, also an arriviste, loses. Tietjens has something valid within him to fall back upon; McKechnie does not. Or, to give a more specific example, when at the end of *A Man Could Stand Up* Tietjens has returned and Valentine goes to his rooms, it should be remembered that the rooms are barren. Sylvia has taken the furniture; the bed and chairs are army equipment. Further, the Armistice celebration is shared only by Valentine and Christopher's army companions; no members of his former world intrude upon it. The volumes teem with similar correspondences, but most important in the above reading is that the climax falls squarely at the end of the series when Sylvia has the Groby Great Tree, the last symbol of pride, felled. England is freed because Christopher is freed, although the freedom is hard won and the implications are grim. Daily life is difficult. Existence is hand to mouth. Christopher deals in antique furniture (he has an infallible eye for the genuine; here he is able to *use* his heritage), which he sells to Americans who wish to buy tradition. The setting may be pastoral, reminiscent of Herbert's parsonage, but we realize that the peace and tranquillity which Herbert felt is not for this century.

The world in which Tietjens moves is crumbling. In England before, during, and after the First World War communication has broken down; old values are no longer applicable; new values have not yet emerged. Ford relentlessly portrays a world with no superstructure, no social, religious, economic, or political constants—a world of anarchy. But Ford, admittedly concerned with the conflict between order and chaos, is also a master of psychological realism, and clearly knows that recognition is the first step toward liberation. But recognition of what? To perceive the disintegration of a social order which one *loves* and which has given strength and body to previous centuries is difficult. This he has done. But today this is no longer enough. It is also necessary to perceive and probe the individual consciousness which has inherited this social order. Experience can be dissected in hundreds of ways; but only if the sensibility which perceives experience is scrutinized as closely and as honestly as the experience itself, only then is integration possible.

The coin is the same. On one side we have read an allegory of social decay. On the other we are concerned first with people, and only secondly with destinies, human or national. The separation is academic since Ford is able to spin the coin so deftly that the readings merge, but if we can hold it still for a moment we see that there are two sides, involving two separate and distinct climaxes.

If *Parade's End* is first an allegory of social decay, the climax must fall on *The Last Post*, and to narrow it down still further, on the felling of the Groby Great Tree. Tietjens:England is freed from the beloved but archaic tradition which has been strangling him. Sylvia, the world of appearances, is now willing to divorce. The book becomes a portrayal of social reality.

But viewed as a study of individual consciousness, it is Christopher Tietjens the man who engages our attention. Keeping this angle of vision, the story builds to a clear and resounding climax in *A Man Could Stand Up* when Christopher comes to the sudden realization that he not only loves but also needs Valentine, and that he will have her. From that point on the pace swiftens and the tone changes to something close to triumph.

The very first scenes of *Some Do Not* put us right in the middle of things with Sylvia proposing to return to Christopher. As their marital situation is revealed, it is clear that the possibility for a real relationship between the two ended long before the volume began. At this point the only basis for their bond is a code of sportsmanship, and Sylvia's chief virtue is a strange kind of self-honesty. Their situation is drawn in the first half of the volume, just as the Edwardian world is drawn in the whole of it. Sylvia makes her vow and lives up to it: 'I'll settle down by that man's side. I'll be as virtuous as any woman. I've made up my mind to it and I'll be it. And I'll be bored stiff for the rest of my life. Except for one thing. I can torment that man. And I'll do it . . . if the worst comes to the worst, I can always drive him silly . . . by corrupting the child!' (p. 41). Father Consett predicts, correctly, that 'her hell on earth will come when her husband goes running, blind, head down, mad after another woman. . . . The more she's made an occupation of torturing him the less right she thinks she has to lose him' (p. 42).

In the second half of the book Tietjens, suffering from partial amnesia, is about to return to the front. We have first a big scene with Sylvia and then a long scene with Valentine. These scenes Ford develops more fully in the next two volumes. We see Sylvia not only as a tormentor but also as a woman plagued by love, hate, and frustration, and *No*

More Parades develops this theme. We see Tietjens begin to turn actively to Valentine, and *A Man Could Stand Up* resolves that situation. Thus the structure of the first three volumes parallels the structure of the first volume which serves as their base. In *Some Do Not*, Ford establishes his world and the centers of conflict; he also intimates the outcome.

The core of *No More Parades* is the relationship with Sylvia, and the volume properly belongs to her. She has followed Christopher to France. She wants to torment him, and she wants to seduce him. She hates him, but she loves him. She is the victim of her own ambivalences as, if we remember Firebaugh, the world may be a victim of its own ambivalences.

We begin the book with Christopher in war, and our sympathy is unhesitatingly with him. Yet when Sylvia finally appears in flesh, not just in Christopher's thoughts, Ford comes up with a brilliant and terrifying piece of writing. He switches to Sylvia, and we begin to view the situation with her eyes. In a passage which is close to stream of consciousness, we are involved in her personal hell of hate, love, and frustrated desire, and at this point—when the reader is most inclined toward sympathy or compassion—Ford allows her her most fiendish scene. Sylvia, waiting for Christopher, remembers

> the white bulldog I thrashed on the night before it died. . . . A tired, silent beast . . . With a fat white behind. . . . Tired out . . . A great, silent beast. . . . And the poor beast had left its kennel to try and be let into the fire. . . . And [I] got the rhinoceros whip and lashed into it. There's a pleasure in lashing into a naked white beast. . . . Obese and silent, like Christopher. . . . They found it dead there in the morning. . . . In thirty degrees of frost with all the blood-vessels exposed on the naked surface of the skin. . . . The last stud-white bulldog of that breed. . . . As Christopher is the last stud-white hope of the Groby Tory breed. . . . Modelling himself on our Lord. . . . But our Lord was never married. He never touched on topics of sex. Good for Him. . . . (pp. 416–17)

It is a horrifying scene, and since we approach it with relative sympathy for Sylvia the shock is heightened. It helps to explain Sylvia, and it also, I think, brings up the question which Robie Macauley poses in his introduction: 'Why is Christopher Tietjens so endlessly persecuted?' (p. x). Sylvia likens Christopher to Christ, with particular reference to her desires and his abstentions. Actually it is only when Christopher is in the army, when he suffers for and with his men, shares the suffering and puts it onto his own shoulders, when, in other words, he identifies with his men and ceases to be the detached observer, that this simile works. Christ, by embracing our sin and our guilt, atones for them. But with Sylvia, as with many of the characters in the Edwardian world who *do* persecute him, Christopher is less of a Christ and more of a Jehovah. 'He was . . . Tietjens of Groby; no man could give him anything, no man could take anything from him' (p. 556). He had an inner code which allowed him to be aloof from the world, from external reality. He did not need it, but—and it is a big but—he was able to judge it. Jehovah, as we know, is a God whom it is easy to fear and easy to hate; if we love him, we do so because he is just and brings order.

In *No More Parades*, Ford not only develops the relationship between Christopher and Sylvia, he resolves it. In a move of desperation she breaks, for the first time, her rule of sportsmanship. She makes a public scandal of a private affair, and in thus trying to force a reaction out of him she breaks the one solid bond which has held them together.

Up to this point Christopher has covered for his wife. The world thinks of him as a libertine, not as a cuckolded husband, and he has preferred it this way. Whether this is due to an ethical code which never permits a man to allow his wife to appear in the wrong, or whether it is easier on the male pride—or both—is a moot point. But now Sylvia, having exploded the myth, robs herself of her only security in him. Although she succeeds in hurting him, she loses him. Christopher is strafed and sent to the front. Death being near, the choice between life and death ceases to be abstract and becomes real. If Christopher chooses life, he must also choose between that which he must have and that which he holds dear but can do without. In *A Man Could Stand Up*, Christopher chooses.

If *No More Parades* belongs to Christopher and Sylvia, *A Man Could Stand Up*, the third volume, belongs to Christopher and Valentine. Here Ford lets them find their way to each other and resolves the triangle. The volume is set at the front where Tietjens is second in command of a battalion awaiting attack. There is mud and endless worry. Communications are breaking down. His colonel has begun to drink and loses control. McKechnie, the only other officer, is belligerent and frenzied. Morale is low. Insanity, heroism, futility mingle. Christopher retains his outer stability but it is here that, fearing madness in a mad world, he again draws on the tradition of the past to help him face a chaotic present, and thinks of George Herbert at his Bemerton parsonage. 'He imagined himself standing up on a little hill, a lean contemplative parson, looking at the land sloping down to Salisbury spire. A large, clumsily bound seventeenth-century testament, Greek, beneath his elbow. . . . Imagine standing up on a hill! It was the un-thinkable thing there!' (p. 567). Later, the acting Sergeant Major echoes the theme: when the war ended a man could stand up on a hill. 'You want to stand up! Take a look around. . . . Like as if you wanted to breathe deep after bein' in a stoopin' posture for a long time!' (p. 570). There follows a lengthy interior monologue which leads Christopher to the sudden realization that he is indeed in love with, needs, and will have Valentine. Here is the climactic turning point in the life of Christopher Tietjens. The war stood between him and Valentine. If the Huns would go home,

> he could be sitting talking to her for whole afternoons. That was what a young woman was for. You seduced a young woman in order to be able to finish your talks with her. You could not do that without living with her. You could not live with her without seducing her: but that was the by-product. The point is that you can't otherwise talk. . . . That in effect was love. It struck him as astonishing. The word was so little in his vocabulary. . . . Love, ambition, the desire for wealth. They were things he had never known of as existing—as capable of existing within him. He had been the Younger Son, loafing, contemptuous, capable, idly contemplating life, but ready to take up the position of the Head of the Family if Death so arranged matters. He had been a sort of eternal Second in Command. (pp. 629-30)

The shock of the war, the exhaustion, the waiting, the alienation from all that had previously surrounded him brings Christopher to the choice between Groby and what Groby represents, and Valentine. One cannot have a mistress at Groby, but since there is an heir and Groby is safe, he is free to go with Valentine. Self-realization loosens the hold of unrealistic conventions and rigid private codes, enabling choice which leads to involvement. In the very beginning of *Some Do Not*, 'as Tietjens saw the world, you didn't "talk". Perhaps you didn't even think about how you felt' (p. 6). Now you do. This scene is the turning point. Until now Tietjens has had little desire to return from the war, but now the desire for life has overcome the wish for death; the passive observer gives way to the active participant. He is still unwilling to divorce; he will be unable to marry Valentine, he will be

living in open defiance of convention, but he will have her; the compli-
cations of a life with Valentine which had seemed so overwhelming
shrink in the light of his realization. When Tietjens is shortly thereafter
unjustly relieved of his command, he nevertheless murmurs, 'It *is* a
land of Hope and Glory!' (p. 644).

Here, then, is our climax. From this point on the tone lightens, the
pace quickens, until we reach the triumphant statement, 'Today the
world changed. Feudalism was finished; its last vestiges were gone. It
held no place for him. He was going—he was damn well going!—to
make a place in it for . . . A man could stand up on a hill, so he and
she could surely get into some hole together' (p. 668). The book ends on
Valentine's thoughts and on an almost unbearably tender note: 'On an
elephant. A dear, mealsack elephant. She was setting out on . . .' (p. 674).

The Last Post, in this reading, becomes a coda. According to Ford
himself, 'the last paragraph of a story should have the effect of what
musicians call a coda—a passage meditative in tone, suited for letting
the reader or hearer gently down from the tense drama of the story, in
which all his senses have been shut up, into the ordinary workaday
world again'.[4] If we substitute the word 'volume' for 'paragraph', we
see the definition fits. *The Last Post* is a necessary and all-embracing
final passage which indicates that although Tietjens may have come to
terms, the terms are difficult. Ford leaves him with his feet on the
ground, but he leaves him in a workaday world in which it will not be
easy to survive. The triumphant note of personal victory which ended
A Man Could Stand Up modulates to the somber tone of daily reality in
The Last Post.

Thus in this reading *Some Do Not* sets the stage, outlines the conflicts,
and suggests the resolution. In *No More Parades* we have Sylvia's last
stand, which is unsuccessful. In *A Man Could Stand Up* we have the final
rejection of Sylvia and the embracing of Valentine. In recognizing his
need, and in being willing to satisfy it, Christopher is also willing and
able to slough off that part of his tradition which has been stifling him.
And in *The Last Post*, where 'the reader is being let down gently from
the tense drama of the story', Ford reweaves all the threads into the
tapestry.

He has created a hero who embodies order and stability, although the
order is in part archaic and therefore debilitating. He then proceeds to
examine his hero with painstaking honesty, and, it should be added,

with gentleness. It is the painful recognition of a series of personal needs which affords Christopher freedom of choice, and he finally chooses to live—integrated but vulnerable—in the twentieth century. Existence is passive. Commitment is active and makes us vulnerable. Order, tradition, and morality are essential, but they must be of our time, and our time excludes parades '... no more parades for you and me any more. Nor for the country ... nor for the world, I dare say ... None ... Gone ... Na poo, finny! No ... more ... parades' (pp. 306–7). Once Christopher accepts this so fully that he applies it to himself as well, he ceases to react and begins to relate. As a result he can accept active involvement with Valentine. This, then, is the other side of the coin, leading to a distinct climax of its own, concentrating on the individual conflicts of a given man, the Last Tory, in a difficult world.

This, too, is a valid reading, but again an incomplete one. Although I have disentangled the two thematic patterns for the sake of discussion, it is only when they are superimposed upon each other that we get the whole of *Parade's End*. But it is a whole in which the climax shifts, and some might argue that this is an artistic flaw. Yet surely it does reflect a world in which sensibility became alienated from the social order, in which external and internal reality were not fused. Ford was able to depict both. It seems fitting that the two themes were brought to separate and distinct climaxes. Whether or not Ford deliberately devised this technique seems immaterial. The fact remains that the technique is there. At the same time, of course, he was successful in presenting his characters simultaneously as real people and as symbols, or allegorical representations—an achievement he shares with many writers of stature.

I have been discussing the four volumes as one structural unit. There are those who feel the premise is false, that these are four separate books about a single hero published over a five-year span. The fact may account for their unevenness, but the position is hardly justifiable. There exists a manuscript version of the scene which Ford had originally intended as the closing of *Some Do Not*.[5] A strong and almost violent scene between Christopher and Sylvia, it ends with Sylvia's last word, 'Paddington'. Sylvia would have departed not only from the apartment but also from Tietjens' life. The book, which begins in a railway carriage, would have ended with the word Paddington. In between we would have seen enough of Valentine to realize that the present stalemate might become the potential resolution. It would have been a tightly structured book, but as it is Ford incorporated the scene into *No More Parades*, sacrificing the structural unity of one volume to the structural unity of three. Ford is a writer who would never let a given scene dominate, but subordinated all his scenes to the creation of one 'effect'. This may be a disturbing technique to those of us who want dramatic explosions to erupt from the page, but it is certainly one way of going about the business. When we accept it as such, we see that the inclusion of the original scene would have sacrificed a larger effect to a dramatic moment, and that *he was clearly planning for the larger effect*.

Regarding *The Last Post*, reference is usually made to Ford's remark that this volume was written in answer to Isabel Patterson's insistence on knowing what became of Tietjens. Perhaps. In his dedication of *A Man Could Stand Up* he does, however, refer to that volume as the third and penultimate. In *The Last Post*, Ford leads us to the allegorical climax and shows us where the threads of allegory end in the tapestry. He also leads us from the internal back to the external. Tietjens is hardly visible (he appears in flesh for only a brief moment). Once the man stood up, Ford shifts back and shows us the world in which he is standing. Although this volume is perhaps the weakest of the four (overly symbolic, some of the interior monologues are plodding affairs at best), it is essential in that it unifies the two patterns and most closely interrelates the two realities. There is little doubt that structurally these volumes do not show the tight and iron control of *The Good Soldier*; but in *Parade's End* Ford paints on a much bigger canvas.

Although rich, complex, and inclusive, *Parade's End* is not a perfect work. I have, however, tried to show that it is an important one. Why? Certainly it is not a new thing to treat both the personal and the broad social spheres of life: Tolstoy did this in *War and Peace*, for example, and Thackeray at least tried it in *Vanity Fair*. The panorama has been coupled with the close-up in numerous novels from *Tom Jones* on. What is noteworthy about Ford's achievement is that he has been able to represent the individual and society from both within and without. The earlier novelists represented individuals *in* society as a matter of course. By the time Ford began to write *Parade's End*, the individual had become alienated from the old social security to such an extent that Ford was forced to try to bridge a chasm grown so deep and wide that few novelists could even see from one side to the other. Alienation had become a matter of course, and Ford's quite modern problem was to present the individual in a stagnant, fast-evaporating pond of received tradition, or in a tradition-less vacuum, without concentrating exclusively on the now fashionable narrow inner focus. He had, that is, to show an individual coming to grips with the new dichotomy of private man and social man, and at the same time to show how the social and private worlds relate. It is a remarkable accomplishment that Ford was able to resolve this complex task.

When we read a contemporary writer to whom we cannot yet apply the test of time, and Ford is certainly contemporary, we must ask how honestly he has perceived his world, how he has reacted to it, and of what possible benefit that reaction is to us. A writer, if he is honest and good, will be able to formulate that which the rest of us may sense with our nerve ends only. Does he, we must therefore ask, enable us to see ourselves or our world more clearly?

With Ford I think we are able to answer yes, and add that he enables us to see ourselves *and* our world more clearly. He probes both internal and external reality. He perceives incisively and without self-pity. Sensibility and experience are combined since he embraces social reality as well as the individual consciousness. In both realms he has tried to separate the fraudulent or archaic from the real, and the recognition of these separations makes for two distinct climaxes.

In *Parade's End*, Ford does not focus on individuals at the expense of society nor on society at the expense of individuals. He does not stay on the periphery of contemporary life, nor does he stay on the periphery of the individual consciousness. He penetrates both. In so doing, his perception and his reaction to it are important to us because the questions which he poses are not yet resolved. They are our questions still.

SOURCE: *Modern Fiction Studies*, IX (1963).

NOTES

1. See, e.g., the first chapter of David Daiches' *The Novel and the Modern World*, rev. ed. (Chicago, 1960).

2. Ford Madox Ford, *Parade's End*, Mid-Century Book Society ed. (New York, 1961) p. 5. [*Editor's note.*] A reprint of Knopf, 1951 ed.

3. Joseph J. Firebaugh, 'Tietjens and the Tradition', *The Pacific Spectator*, VI (Winter 1952) 23–32.

4. Ford Madox Ford, 'Conrad and the Sea', *Portraits from Life* (Chicago, [1960]) pp. 82–3.

5. I am indebted to Professor Frank MacShane, University of California at Berkeley, for making this information available to me.

MELVIN SEIDEN

Persecution and Paranoia in
Parade's End (1966)

'THERE you are working yourself to death to save the nation with a wilderness of cats and monkeys howling and squalling your personal reputation away. . . . It was Dizzy himself said these words to me . . . ,' Mrs Wannop explains to Christopher Tietjens. Mrs Wannop, a novelist and mother of the young girl with whom Christopher is beginning to fall in love, goes on to relate Disraeli's comment to Christopher's problems: 'The only thing that matters is to do good work. . . . You'll find consolation in that. And you'll live it all down. Or perhaps you won't. . . .' Though there are tears in his eyes, Christopher replies with characteristic gallantry and phlegm, 'What I'm concerned for at the moment is not my reputation, but your daughter Valentine's.'[1]

Tietjens ought to be concerned for his reputation, since he is at this early point in the story and is about to become increasingly a man who is consistently misunderstood, calumniated, and scorned. Dizzy's remark to Mrs Wannop is an accurate description of the perplexities of Ford's bedeviled hero in *Parade's End*.

It would be a considerable undertaking for the critic, text in hand, to draw up a complete list of the persecutions endured by Tietjens. It is impossible to remember them all, but some of the calumnies are unforgettable. It is said that Tietjens sold his wife to another man and lives off these 'immoral earnings'; that Valentine Wannop is his mistress, as is a Mrs Duchemin who is in fact the mistress of his friend Vincent Macmaster; that his disgraceful behavior caused the suicide of his father; that he has even stolen his wife's bed linen, a charge suggesting that the whole range from the sublime to the ridiculous is covered by the attacks on Tietjens' reputation. A catalogue entitled, 'What Erroneously is Said or Believed about Tietjens and by Whom' would be a formidable one. In it would appear Tietjens' wife, brother, father, commanding officer (also his godfather), his friend and protégé, Macmaster, and numerous minor figures who have had only the most peripheral relationships with him; even Valentine believes ill of him briefly.

So much malice, so many wildly wrong beliefs and confidently asserted 'facts', such virulence in besmirching 'personal reputation'— these are the 'improbabilities' that are plausible in the outrageous world of comedy. It is the fate of the comic lout to suffer and the comic rogue to thrive on such absurd misconstructions of fact and error of opinion. About the character of Tom Jones, for example, some of his friends and most of his enemies are deceived in the way in which the world misunderstands Tietjens.

But Tietjens is not a comic figure and *Parade's End* is not a comedy in any commonly accepted sense of the term. The stakes are too high, the consequences of the plots against Tietjens are too painful to permit us to enjoy his disasters with that comforting sense of security which is an essential condition for comedy.

Why does Ford heap so many indignities upon the head of poor Christopher?

Most obviously—and for purposes antithetical to a comic effect— to authenticate the claims of Tietjens' moral earnestness. To the extent that Tietjens' stern moral code brings ignominy upon him the code is established as worthy of our respect. The malice he inspires in others is for us a sign of his deserving to be respected. The contempt of others nourishes our affection, their irritation feeds our fondness, the corrupt world gives him his crown of thorns and we give him his proper title. The more adamant Christopher's pursuit of virtue the more it must come to pass that even decent men like Christopher's brother Mark and sick souls like Mrs Duchemin and Sylvia Tietjens will misunderstand and loathe Tietjens' virtue. Mrs Duchemin is driven by spite, hysterical envy, and hypocrisy. But though Mark Tietjens is in many ways cut from the same cloth as Christopher, his own stiff rectitude causes him to misunderstand it in his brother.

Tietjens is made to suffer so that something like tragic status may be bestowed upon him. He suffers stoically. Wise, perceptive, and express- ive though he is in many ways, Christopher has too much of the milord's *sang-froid* to be able to express his sufferings openly.

But though in literature as in life to live inflexibly by high moral standards is to court disaster, this verity gives too simple an account of

Tietjens' fate. A certain opportunism often complicates the process whereby we make moral inferences in literature. It is the opportunism of wanting to have it both ways. Witnessing the spectacle of the good man at bay in an evil world, we enjoy the righteousness of condemning those who afflict him, yet we participate covertly in the hostility that motivates these afflictions. 'Poor fellow,' we say; but if we listen carefully to the dialogue of our responses we will detect another voice that says, 'But the bloody fool deserves it'.

To be sure, we respond feelingly to the many injustices endured by Christopher. Yet we recognize that not even Sylvia Tietjens, who is the most relentless (though also the most admirable) of his enemies, is totally unjust to Christopher. To her he is intolerable, to us he is lovable; yet we must confess that we too would find him intolerable as husband or friend. Our hearts go out to him but opportunism permits us to believe without any sense of being caught in a contradiction that a would-be saint must suffer the afflictions that confer sanctity. 'How else', we cynically ask, 'would he know and we recognize that he is a righteous man? How else can he be confirmed in his righteousness if not through the slings and arrows of contumely?' Watching Tietjens struggle against a malevolent world, we are not wholly free from the scorn and contempt of that malevolence. Sympathetic though we are to his lofty ideals, we are nevertheless irritated by the extravagant claims of his virtues. There is of course something inhuman in his sanctity.

Of General Campion, Christopher's most amusing yet not quite ingenuous nor altogether harmless persecutor, we can say that it is unthinkable that he would *not* misunderstand, resent, and feel himself obliged to oppose Tietjens' queer morality. Yet we share his exasperation when he asks, 'What the hell are you?' and his description of Tietjens elicits our smiling assent:

> You're not a soldier. You've got the makings of a damn good soldier. You amaze me at times. Yet you're a disaster; you are a disaster to every one who has to do with you. You are as conceited as a hog; you are as obstinate as a bullock. . . . You drive me mad. . . .

But that smile of ours turns bitter as Campion goes on to a half truth as bad as a lie: 'And you have ruined the life of that beautiful woman [Sylvia]. . . . For I maintain she once had the disposition of a saint.'[2]

In this brilliant scene in which Tietjens tries and yet does not really try to defend himself against the fantastic charges brought against him by General Campion—the General's terse list will give us a taste of the tragi-comic flavor of the accusations: ' "Colonel's horse: Sheets: Jesus Christ: Wannop girl: Socialism?" '—the ironies are not solely at the expense of the befuddled Campion. The ironies undercut Tietjens' suffering and transform what would otherwise be simple pathos into a response that reflects our impatience with Tietjens' perverse martyrdom.

It is of course characteristic of irony to cut down pretensions, to question motives, to cast aspersions upon rectitude, to diminish the grand and raise up the lowly, to take seriously what no merely sound mind doubts and to doubt the indubitable. Like Iago, irony is nothing if not critical. But for the writer to be able to subject one of his characters to the debunking of irony he must be capable of seeing him in all his naked otherness. He must be able to see the character as he cannot see himself, as we rarely see ourselves unless by some miracle which defies psychic phenomena as they are now understood there should happen to exist someone who is both schizoid and insightful, a schizophrenic who in one of his persons is able clearly to understand what that other person is. The schizophrenic has no such clarity of vision, nor can most of us, who are not, turn the full force of ironical scrutiny upon ourselves.

The novelist who wrote *The Good Soldier* was above all an ironist. The voice of Dowell, narrator and protagonist, is the only clear voice we are permitted to hear; we have only his report of what happened and why. Opinions, surmises, and the responses of others are filtered through his sensibility. The result is a tightly unified irony. Dowell is the unwitting ironist and he himself is the object of that corroding irony. It is an exercise in self exposure. When it has been played out there is nothing that has not been eaten away by the irony. Everything is dubious, even the comfortable refuge of dubiety that Dowell retreats to so often and symptomatically. It is all oppressively murky. The brilliant clarity of the parts adds up to a terrible darkness.

Dowell is—and not altogether convincingly—an American. This in itself suggests the emotional distance between the writer and his character; or at least, the distance that Ford wants to put between Dowellism in himself and his understanding of it.

Ford cannot have wanted to try to repeat the success of this *tour de force.* Even if he had, the course of his life and the experiences of the war had given him a point of view that was incompatible with the relentless and perhaps too facile irony of *The Good Soldier.* Ford was not capable of crushing Tietjens with the kind of irony he had directed against Dowell—either not capable, which makes it a biographical matter, or not desirous of doing so. In any case, in *Parade's End* sympathetic pathos is stronger and more pervasive than irony.

Tietjens is more intelligent and sensitive than Dowell. He is never self-deceived in the obviously crippling ways in which Dowell's obtuseness causes him to be misled and confused. Dowell is entangled in one situation, an enormously complex entanglement to be sure, but single, discrete, and contained, whereas Tietjens' affairs embroil him in the operations of a whole society; and even if we argue that, like Dowell, Tietjens is self-victimized, it is clear that he is primarily the victim of the malevolence of others. Dowell is destroyed; it could not have been otherwise because he has destroyed himself. The 'happy ending' of *The Last Post* is possible and does not ring false because Tietjens' problems are in great measure due to others; and when his enemies have changed, as Sylvia does through a kind of religious conversion, or find themselves no longer wanting or being able to harm him in the differently constituted society that emerges after the First World War, it becomes possible for Tietjens to salvage his life through marriage (without benefit of clergy) to Valentine and a new career outside of upper-class society as a dealer in second-hand furniture. And since the domestic idyl of the fourth volume of the tetralogy (not perfectly idyllic to be sure) is the direction in which the action has been moving, it is evident that the rigorous irony of *The Good Soldier* could not have served Ford's purposes in *Parade's End.*

Tietjens is more alive than Dowell has ever been. He thinks, he acts, he suffers; he has noble purposes; he is not trapped, as Dowell is, in a prison of his own making, unable to communicate, unable to achieve manhood, unable to find a convincing identity. If Dowell is a symbol of a sick society, Tietjens is a saint—or a saint manqué; it does not matter; he is effective enough in any case—whose moral health exposes society's disease. If Dowell's death-in-life registers the symptoms of this disease, Tietjens' life is a successful struggle to ward it off. What Dowellism there is in him is only a fever that indicates resistance to the disease. The most revealing single difference between the two is that

Tietjens is attractive to women; he is a man and Dowell is a sexless
nursemaid.

John Rodker's witty remark about *The Good Soldier*—'the best
French novel in the English language'—will not do for *Parade's End*.
The tetralogy needs to be praised in other terms. We may find it more
ambitious and interesting than *The Good Soldier*, but we must concede
that it lacks the formal perfection (the prideful and possibly shallow
brilliance, some of us might say) of the earlier novel.

We may discern a paradox in the kind of achievement represented by
The Good Soldier. Nothing could be more 'personal' than this imposition
of one voice, one mind, one set of values upon the materials of a novel.
It is exceedingly difficult and perhaps impossible for us to penetrate
Dowell's sensibility and reach the firm ground of an objective reality
about which we can make reliable statements. The personalism of
the strictly first-person point of view thus leads to an austere impersonal-
ity. There is of course an author manipulating Dowell's manipulation
of the narrative, but we cannot determine much about this transaction.
We can find out almost nothing about Ford's moral values. These are
not merely concealed; in a very real sense they do not exist. We must
make the best of what is given to us by the quirky, inadequate, and
highly unreliable perceptions of Dowell's mind.

Parade's End bears the stamp of Ford's intervening predilections and
preoccupations; *The Good Soldier* does not. The style of the tetralogy,
varied and uneven though it is, permits us to hear the voice of Ford
beneath that of Tietjens. Ford's relationship to *Parade's End* may be
compared to that of D. H. Lawrence to his novels; and if the success
of *The Good Soldier* is in the tradition of the art of Austen, James, and
the Joyce of *Dubliners*, whatever Ford may have achieved or failed to
achieve in *Parade's End* will have to be judged by the kinds of standards
that are appropriate to novelists like Lawrence, Eliot, Dostoevsky, and
Melville. We are of course making the distinction between the art of
the novel 'pure and impure', between 'the novel as poem' and the
doctrinal or thesis novel, between the novel of sensibility and the novel
of ideas, between the novel of suggestion and the novel of statement,
between the novel which imposes upon itself rigorous formal restric-
tions and the novel that stoops to explain, analyze, and discuss the issues
raised in it. These antitheses are too neat, and it would be foolish to
expect the craftsman who wrote *The Good Soldier* to have lost or

thrown away his art and to have written anything so formless as is suggested by our simplistic formulas for the 'impure' novel. Nevertheless, these dichotomies are useful in giving us a sense of the differences between *The Good Soldier* and *Parade's End*.

Lawrence is an extreme case in which personal vision becomes a messianic passion, but it is true of all novelists who foresake Keats' impersonal 'negative capability' that they stake the whole life of their work on the force and persuasiveness of the vision it asserts. *Parade's End* is no exception. Our responses to Tietjens require that we assent to moral, sexual, and political ideas which, though less stridently or baldly expressed than those of Lawrence, are no less determining.

E. V. Walter has written an interesting analysis of Ford's ideas.[3] He makes a good case for Ford as a critic of England's social and moral disorders. He argues plausibly that 'the politics of the tetralogy is an aspect as essential to an understanding of Ford's authorship as is his craft'. In examining the politics of *Parade's End* Mr Walter does not hesitate to impute Tietjens' views to Ford, an identification that cannot be condemned as illegitimate in this case. Illuminating though Mr Walter is in dealing with the doctrinal significance of Tietjens' career, he tends to reduce the complexities of character to the excessively clear-cut and unequivocal pattern of the dialectic of ideas, so that in remarks like the following the conflicts become tidier and more rational than they strike us as being in the tetralogy:

> The all but destructive effect of the war on the mind of Tietjens represents its effect on aristocracy and tradition itself. . . . Feudalism survives under ground with Tietjens, but in the world it is finished [after Armistice Day].[4]

The men and women who seek to destroy Tietjens are only incidentally the impersonal agents of the social forces described by Mr Walter. Ford's main point is not the socio-political observation that men of good will find themselves alienated and driven underground by a moribund civilization, true though this is. Ford insists on something that is less ideological and more emotionally and personally charged. It is that this extraordinarily idiosyncratic man, Christopher Tietjens, arouses the animosity of others not only because he is whole and they are, as Robie Macauley put it, 'fragmentary people, uncertain, confused, without values,'[5] but more importantly because their inability to know what to make of him goads them into vindictive hatred. Christopher is too

genuinely democratic to be understandable as an aristocrat, too passionate to be the Tory squire, too rooted in his class loyalties and the ethics
of the public schoolboy to be the deliberate renegade to these traditions,
yet too much the radical despite himself to be able to mesh smoothly
with the habits and prejudices of any group, class, or profession; so that
it is the totality of these contradictions that is the main fact about
Tietjens. Neither we nor Tietjens' enemies can make out clearly who or
what he *is*, and it is all the more difficult to determine what he represents
socially or politically. To paraphrase Churchill: Christopher Tietjens is
an enigma inside an anomaly, and this is why he invites the crucifixion
that the world willingly bestows upon him. If indeed he has in some
measure attained to the Anglican sainthood which he defines as 'the
quality of being in harmony with your own soul,' that agitated (and
agitating) harmony is an affront to those who must endure it.

In *A Man Could Stand Up* we find Christopher reminiscing about
the inglorious death of a Major Perowne:

> The Providence for Perowne! For, when he was dug out after, next night
> having been buried in going up into the trenches, they said, he had a smile
> like a young baby's on his face. He didn't have long to wait and died with
> a smile on his face . . . nothing having so much become him during the
> life as . . . well, a becoming smile! (p. 569)

Why the smile on Perowne's face? It is the result, apparently, of
Christopher's having 'persuade[d] the unhappy mortal called Perowne
that death was not a very dreadful affair. . . . He had enough intellectual
authority to persuade the fellow with his glued-down black hair that
Death supplied His own anaesthetics.'

Who is this Major Perowne? He is 'one of those individuals who have
no history, no strong proclivities, nothing. . . .'[6] He is someone with
whom Sylvia Tietjens once had a meaningless affair, 'an oaf' who
attempts to whine his way back into Sylvia's bed when she comes to the
front in France to torment Christopher. The consequences of this
attempt, which fails, are described in an episode (*No More Parades*, pp.
459ff.) reminiscent of the hilarious mis-matings and mistaken entrances
and exits of the famous night at the Upton inn of *Tom Jones*.

It is extraordinary that Christopher should be comforting this man to
relieve his fear of death. 'During life he had seemed a worried, fussing
sort of chap'—this is Tietjens' final thought about the man who has

cuckolded him and brought disgrace to him as a result of the contre-
temps in Sylvia's hotel room.

We may be tempted to suppose that Christopher's ministrations are
comic, a variation on the standard joke about the complaisant (French)
husband's friendly comments to his wife's lover. But if preparing one's
wife's lover for death with the solacing thought that 'Death supplied
His own anaesthetics' is grotesque, it is not quite comic. Perowne
almost becomes for us, as he seems to be for Christopher, an object of
pathos. If Christopher 'understands' and we are not given the opportun-
ity to detest so unredeemed an oaf as Perowne, then the charity that
imposes so strict a tolerance upon us is likely to end by destroying the
health of our emotions. That may be what Ford is trying to tell us—
that Tietjens' saintliness is a self-inflicted wound. But is it?

Here is Tietjens' view of himself:

> They've got me out, with all sorts of bad marks against me. They'll pursue
> me, systematically. .... You see in such a world as this, an idealist—or
> perhaps it's only a sentimentalist—must be stoned to death. He makes the
> others so uncomfortable. He haunts them at their golf.[7]

The tone of this characteristic remark is one of sweet reasonableness.
Tietjens recognizes that he must be loathed; but he does not excoriate
those who hate him. If it is because he is a sentimentalist that he 'must
be stoned to death', the emotionless tolerance with which he observes
his fate is itself a kind of sentimentality. He cannot or will not be
indignant. He accepts stoically Macmaster's having stolen his work and
used it for advancement in government service, just as he is able to
reflect wisely and dispassionately upon Sylvia's 'sex ferocity'—and
there is, we are sure, something terribly wrong about the emotional
consequences of this ambition of his to 'be able to touch pitch and not
be defiled. That he knew [Tietjens reflects] marked him off as belonging
to the sentimental branch of humanity. He couldn't help it: Stoic or
Epicurean; Caliph in the harem or Dervish desiccating in the sand; one
or the other you must be.'[8] That is precisely the right word—desiccating—for Christopher's relentless and stoical charity.

His phrase, 'they've got me out', suggests, moreover, the standard
American expression associated with paranoia: 'they're out to get me',
and we must face squarely, though Ford does not, the problem of
paranoia in *Parade's End*.

The paranoiac imputes sinister motives to innocent words and deeds; or, if by word or deed the other person has in fact expressed hostility but, as is so often the case, only momentarily and impulsively, the paranoiac detects in this evidence of a deep and abiding design to do him harm. The paranoiac, through his fantasies of hatred in others ('projection' in psychoanalytical terminology) destroys or does serious psychic harm to himself through his own very real hatred of these fearful 'others'.

This description does not fit the psychology of Tietjens. If we assume, as we must, that his freedom from self-lacerating bitterness and hatred is genuine, then he would appear to be the very opposite of the paranoiac: the man who achieves immunity from the ravages of hatred through forgiveness of his enemies—'others' who, it must be stressed, are presented to us by Ford as being as wicked as Tietjens takes them to be. There is no question that the malevolent persecutions of Tietjens are 'real'; the tetralogy documents them in great detail.

Point by point, incident by incident, explanation by explanation, these persecutions are plausible. But it is just this plausibility that arouses our suspicions. The web of conspiracy against Tietjens has the excessively logical, almost mathematical coherence that we have been taught by psychoanalysis to recognize as another symptom of paranoia: the irrationality of pseudo-rationality.

Now this symptom does fit Tietjens' case—more precisely, Ford's; since the explanations have a persistent and strong authorial sanction, the charge of paranoia is primarily against Ford's vision of the human condition. If the circumstances and justifications[9] connected with Tietjens' afflictions had been less clear and explicit; if Ford had permitted us, whether by the greater use of irony or through the insights of others, to find a vantage point from which we could corroborate, qualify, or in some way assess independently the Tietjens-Ford insistence upon a nearly universal conspiracy to defame and hunt down Tietjens, we would not be forced to complain that all of this is too intellectually systematic to be emotionally palatable.

Discussing the genesis of Tietjens in his imagination, Ford observes in *It Was the Nightingale*:

> If he is the sort of man to have put up with the *treacheries* of others his interests at home will suffer from *treasons*; . . . if he is a man destined to be *betrayed* by women his women will *betray* him exaggeratedly and without

shame. For all these vicissitudes will be exaggerated by the more strident note that in time of war gets into both speeches and events. . . . And he is indeed, then, *homo duplex*. . . . [10] (Italics mine.)

This is the same reasonable tone we find in the novels, but the harping on treason and betrayal suggests a bitterness which, if Ford dared to express it, might well erupt into savage hatred. As for his explanation of the hero's being betrayed 'exaggeratedly', the logic of the connection between war conditions and whatever it is that makes a woman betray a man is not altogether clear.

We do not require biographical evidence, plentiful though it is, to lead us to the disturbing insight that something akin to a paranoid vision informs the world of *Parade's End*. Tietjens' hunger for sanctity is Ford's, in the sense that Ford will not allow either Tietjens or his readers the gratification of a just and proper indignation. But Ford cannot cheat himself or us of this catharsis without paying a price. By a kind of compensatory logic he multiplies inordinately the infamies suffered by Tietjens, the point being that, though Tietjens always forgives, the world never relents in its hostility toward him. The proof as it were of Tietjens' moral sanity is that 'everyone's out to get him'.[11] But lacking the emotional and moral satisfaction that catharsis would afford us, we find ourselves wondering whether this vast conspiracy of evil does not reveal something quite different from what Ford appears to have intended it to show. Does Ford realize how much he asks of us by insisting that so much malevolence is dedicated to the destruction of one eccentric, harmless Yorkshire gentleman?

There are many references to Christopher's being a little 'dotty', as was his mother, a saintly woman, we are told. But the implication, surely, is that if he is 'dotty' it is only in the sense in which pure souls are thought to be so by corrupt men. Ford relishes Tietjens' eccentricities: his pointlessly encyclopedic memory, his odd Anglican deference to Roman Catholicism, his unashamed snobberies, his radical Toryism, and above all, his absolute indifference to what the world makes of him. Ford encourages us to be amused at these eccentricities; we can smile at those traits that cause him to be slandered and attacked. What we must not do is doubt the reality or seriousness of the world's conspiracy to destroy Christopher Tietjens. We are not invited to be amused by *that*.

So that we are not dealing with the question of paranoia in Tietjens. Nothing in the tetralogy indicates that he is to be seen as suffering from delusions of persecution. We may think that he is, but Ford's view of the reality of these persecutions is no different from Tietjens'. Clearly Ford is not dealing with Tietjens as a kind of case study in paranoia. *Parade's End* (happily) is not that kind of 'modern' novel that relies on our sophisticated psychological knowledge to permit us 'to see through' apparent nobility of character and aim to a 'reality' of neurotic deception as the mainspring of behavior. Even in *The Good Soldier* the critical irony does not go so far as to become a psychological exposé.

Yet one of Ford's most intelligent critics, Carol Ohmann, is guilty of the error of interpreting Tietjens in this modernist fashion. She tries to persuade us that in *A Man Could Stand Up* Tietjens experiences an 'inner chaos' so intense as to induce in him what Mrs Ohmann describes as but does not term paranoia:

> With its passion for certainty, the mind as Ford creates it tends to construct design where no design exists. And in moments of strain and misfortune, the mind tends to construct a malevolent picture of the world. . . .[12]

The evidence she cites is from an episode in which Tietjens is observing the activities of the German soldiers moving about on no man's land:

> He sees 'shadows like the corrugations of photographs of the moon' (*MCSU*, p. 549). He thinks, for a moment, that a number of wet trenching sacks are men 'creeping up' (*MCSU*, p. 549). And he transforms the mists above the German lines into gigantic specters.[13]

Mrs Ohmann writes, 'he thinks'; Ford wrote, 'his stomach said'. Christopher knows the difference between what the pictures appear to be and what they are; and Ford wants us to be aware of Christopher's awareness of the difference. Perhaps, as Mrs Ohmann asserts, 'Tietjens has begun to cross the boundary between perception and hallucination'. But Christopher knows where the boundary is and when he has crossed it.

Earlier, Mrs Ohmann had said, 'The worst of his [Tietjens'] ordeal under fire will be his mind's capacity to attend on its own disorders.' But as she makes out a case for virtual insanity in Tietjens, she seems to forget this significant point.

Summing up Christopher's impressions of the German artillery strafe, Mrs Ohmann says, 'The pattern here, of course, is inference. But it is inference running wild, building a skyscraper on a ludicrously shallow basis of fact.' To show how wrong Christopher's surmises are Mrs Ohmann observes that, 'Before the end of Chapter I [Part Two, of *A Man Could Stand Up*], Tietjens has inferred that the enemy attack might just as well have originated in Whitehall as Unter den Linden.'[14] To support her contention that Christopher is out of touch with reality at this point, Mrs Ohmann links Tietjens with the officer McKechnie who 'in one of his recurrent moments of madness says, "Our headquarters are full of Huns doing the Huns' work" (*NMP*, p. 304).' Apparently Mrs Ohmann understands Tietjens' mind to be operating paranoiacally in the surmise that the German attack conceals devious purposes, probably Whitehall's; and in this, she believes, Tietjens is deluded in the same way as the mad McKechnie.

However, the point is made unambiguously, authoritatively, and often that the war effort *is* being sabotaged or betrayed by Whitehall.

> All these men given into the hands of the most cynically carefree intriguers in long corridors who made plots that harrowed the hearts of the world. (*NMP*, p. 296.)

> But who was going to be impressed [by the German strafe]? Of course our legislators with the stewed-pear brains running about the ignoble corridors. ... Or, of course, our own legislators might have been trying a nice little demonstration in force, equally idiotic somewhere else, to impress someone just as unlikely to be impressed. ... (*MCSU*, pp. 562–3.)

Scheming politicians who subvert military goals to immoral political ends, the resentment felt by the civilian for the soldier and which gets expressed as hostility to the soldier as well as to his aims—these notions, unmistakably, are not presented by Ford as the paranoia of battle-fatigue, what Mrs Ohmann calls 'inference running wild'; they are indeed one of the central themes of *Parade's End*, often expressed by Tietjens when, we are to understand, he is thinking most penetratingly about the war and its significance.

It is someone like the corrupt Edith Ethel Duchemin who speaks for and shares the opinions of 'those swine in their corridors'.[15] And Christopher, surely, is right, we are to think, when he says, 'Now the swine were starving the poor devils in the trenches'. Even Sylvia tells Christopher what he already knows or is soon to find out, that 'all the men who aren't in the army hate all the men that are'.

Proof of the correctness of Tietjens' surmises about civilian duplicity is the betrayal of France by the too mild and generous treatment of Germany by England at the end of the war. In disgust, Mark Tietjens withdraws both from government service and the world; he pledges himself to silence, a vow that he steadfastly honors except for one touching moment toward the end of *The Last Post* where he speaks to Valentine. Were there any doubt as to whether we are to accept Tietjens' opinions about Whitehall's guilt, Ford's remarks on this subject in *It Was the Nightingale* would be decisive:

> He [Tietjens] was to be aware that in all places where they managed things from Whitehall down to brigade headquarters a number of things would be badly managed—the difference being that in Whitehall the mismanagement would be so much the result of jealousies that it would have the aspect of the most repellent *treachery* (pp. 217–18; italics mine).

He also speaks of the returning soldiers as 'wanderers coming back to find our settlements occupied by a vindictive and savage tribe . . . our places were taken by strangers' (p. 64). Then, to dramatize his point, Ford tells an anecdote, apocryphal no doubt, which contrasts the humane behavior of the civilized French police who indulge the misbehavior of their veterans with that of English law which, after the war, expressed 'that savage, that hysterical determination to extirpate—as rats—the men to whom the very same public had been on its knees but a few months before . . .' (p. 67). Poor Ford! He seems more pitiable in his hysteria than the returning soldier.

True, Christopher suffers from hallucinations at the front. After the war he finds himself (as Ford said he found himself) without memory. From these aberrations, recognized by Ford and Tietjens for what they are, Tietjens recovers; he recovers from these psychic ills just as he is to recover from the afflictions of society and salvage what remains useful to him in his old life by beginning a new one with Valentine. But since neither Christopher not Ford understands that imputing a vast conspiracy to society is a kind of paranoia, Christopher cannot be made to recover from an 'illness' whose existence is not in the least suspected by his creator. It is not, therefore, Tietjens' opinions that are mistaken but the subtle reading which takes them to be so. These opinions are not evidence of psychic disorder in Tietjens. On the subject of the civilian betrayal of the military, Tietjens speaks for Ford. We may indeed find Christopher's notions repugnant, but if we do, we must direct that distaste to the mind and opinions of Ford.

Ford's intentions are perfectly clear, and we need not be intimidated by a so-called 'fallacy' that assures us that we may not speak of a writer's intentions. What Whitehall does or tries to do to the British Army and its Allies is, unmistakably, a thematic parallel to the crimes committed against Tietjens—macrocosm and microcosm, the agonies of a nation crippled by cultural paresis and Tietjens' 'lasting tribulation —with a permanent shackle and ball on his leg' (*Nightingale*, p. 209). Tietjens' 'inner chaos' gives him an insight into a national malevolence that he has experienced in a variety of different forms as a civilian; and that macrocosmic evil, symbolized by the betrayals hatched in White-hall's corridors, is meant to be every bit as real as the many wicked deeds done to Tietjens before and after the war.

In the Joseph Conrad memoir, Ford observes:

> With the novel you can do anything: you can inquire into every department of life, you can explore every department of thought. The one thing that you can not do is to propagandise. . . . You must not, as author, utter any views. . . . You must not, however humanitarian you may be, over-elaborate the fear felt by a coursed rabbit. (p. 213.)

Christopher Tietjens is Ford's coursed rabbit, and there can be no doubt about the author's humanitarian feelings for him. But Ford exercises a tight control on these feelings, just as he represses passion in Tietjens. Ford is too much the old pro to make the mistake of the in-experienced autobiographical novelist who creates an obvious and indulgent bond between himself and his hero. Ford rarely allows his prose, which is bright, genial, and urbane, to swell with a passion commensurate with the pain of the evil endured by Tietjens. The strains are enormous—on Christopher, who cannot strike out against those who torment him; on Ford, who masks deep resentments behind the bravado of his rather cheerful style; and on us, for we are asked both to grant the ubiquity of malevolence and, apparently, to accept it as dispassion-ately as Tietjens does. And all this containment does not leave us with a sense of a serene Shakespearean ripeness having been achieved but the very opposite. Out of the tension between the apparent equanimity of the prose and the thrust of our partisan (and 'humanitarian') feelings on Tietjens' behalf there arises a deep and moving pathos. Ford makes us

feel the fear felt by his coursed rabbit, however much his cool prose
seeks or pretends to seek to put us off.

In the final moments of *The Last Post* Ford allows nonchalance and
constraint to give way at last to the overt expression of powerful
emotion. Sylvia, through a kind of religious conversion, fights free of
her compulsion to torment Christopher and Valentine, the woman who
has displaced her. Mark, seeing Sylvia now so abjectly defanged, over-
comes his loathing for her and thinks, 'Poor bitch! Poor bitch!' Valentine
is able to get beyond awed admiration and unacknowledged hatred of
Sylvia to a genuine and womanly sympathy. It is a scene rich in sentiment fully earned and not in the least sentimental. For Sylvia, Mark,
and Valentine the tyranny of rancor is ended; and even if they have
achieved something less than the serenity which genuine catharsis
can confer, they have been urged and perfected by the release of honest
feeling.

Ford denies Tietjens this blessedness. Tietjens, who is notably absent
throughout the whole of *The Last Post*, arrives on the scene only after
the emotions of the others have exhausted themselves. His only
comment is the bitter one to Mark, 'Half Groby wall is down. Your
bedroom's wrecked. I found your case of sea-birds thrown on a rubble
heap.' Then, 'heavily, like a dejected bulldog, Christopher made for
the gate'.[16] Christopher, who has always refused to allow himself to
express passion, is denied by Ford the healing knowledge that his
worst enemy has capitulated. Sylvia has cast out the devil that has
goaded her into self-contempt, hatred, and violence; and though we
know this, Tietjens does not. If the central inquiry of *Parade's End* is
into the hunger for sanctity and the denials entailed by feeding that
hunger, it is not surprising that Ford should deny Tietjens the final
redemption of liberating passion. Ford's own hunger for artistic
integrity will not permit him to grant Tietjens his release. The principle
that asserts, 'You must not over-elaborate the fear felt by a coursed
rabbit', requires that Ford keep Tietjens in bondage to his constraints.
To do otherwise would be to forfeit the authenticity that both Ford
and Tietjens have achieved at great cost.

SOURCE: *Criticism*, VIII (summer 1966).

NOTES

1. *Some Do Not* in *Parade's End* (New York, 1950) pp. 118–19.

2. *No More Parades*, p. 481.

3. *New Republic* (26 March 1956) pp. 17–19.

4. Ibid., p. 17.

5. 'Introduction', *Parade's End*, p. xii.

6. *No More Parades*, p. 387.

7. *Some Do Not*, p. 237.

8. Ibid., p. 187.

9. In *Joseph Conrad* (Boston, 1924) pp. 218ff, Ford makes of the mystic word 'justification' a literary principle: 'Before everything a story must convey a sense of inevitability: that which happens in it must seem to be the only thing that could have happened. . . . It must be inevitable, because of his character, because of his ancestry, because of past illness or on account of the gradual coming together of the thousand small circumstances by which Destiny who is inscrutable and august, will push us into one certain predicament.'

10. *It Was the Nightingale* (Philadelphia and London, 1933) p. 217.

11. In his Introduction to *Parade's End*, Robie Macauley asks, 'Why is Christopher Tietjens so endlessly persecuted?' His answer seems to be in the following comment: 'The intolerable fact to her [Sylvia] is that he is sane. And some of this terror at Tietjens is shared by everyone around. They are fragmentary people, uncertain, confused, without values. They sense that Tietjens belongs to a moral frame of reference that both makes the world intelligible and wards off its shocks. To their jumbled and neurotic lives he stands as a reproach, and they must destroy him if possible' (p. xii).

12. *Ford Madox Ford* (Middletown, Conn., 1964) p. 160.

13. Ibid., p. 158.

14. Ibid., p. 159.

15. She says, 'It is imperative that these fellows [men like Christopher, i.e., soldiers] should not have the higher command. It would pander to their insane spirit of militarism. They *must* be hindered' (*SDN*, p. 258.)

16. *The Last Post*, p. 835.

HUGH KENNER

The Poetics of Speech (1970)

IF Ford and Eliot talked it is not recorded (though they must have; surely they must have); and you will search the Index and the Reading Lists in *The March of Literature* in vain for any reference to the poet of Prufrock. Twenty years ago in Washington I questioned Ezra Pound about this, and received two observations: that Ford was 'the only one who foresaw the consequences of Eliot becoming a literary dictator', and that Ford apparently thought 'Prufrock' the kind of thing you could write in twenty minutes. The good parts, we may add upon further reflection, for the admired parts of 'Prufrock' Ford would have considered bad parts:

> And the afternoon, the evening, sleeps so peacefully!
> Smoothed by long fingers,
> Asleep ... tired ... or it malingers
> Stretched on the floor, here beside you and me.

'What could really be worse in the way of uncertain definition,' Ford wrote of two lines of Tennyson's—

> All round the coast the languid air did swoon,
> Breathing like one that hath a weary dream.

For just consider, he said, what it really means. 'Did the air actually snort and grind its teeth as do those who suffer from a nightmare?'[1] Similarly, we can imagine him asking, did the afternoon, the evening (and which, pray, is Tom talking about?) really undergo in that parlor the stroking of feminine fingers? And can a time of day be said to 'malinger'? Or weigh the opening of 'A Game of Chess' in *The Waste Land* against the criteria by which Ford isolates Tennyson's inattention to sentence structure, or his 'imprecise or duplicated images'.

> In vials of ivory and coloured glass
> Unstoppered, lurked her strange synthetic perfumes,
> Unguent, powdered, or liquid—troubled, confused
> And drowned the sense in odours; stirred by the air
> That freshened from the window, these ascended
> In fattening the prolonged candle-flames,
> Flung their smoke into the laquearia,
> Stirring the pattern on the coffered ceiling.

—One backboneless sentence; and what are 'these'? The odours? And if so how do the odours fatten the candle-flames and fling their smoke? Is not that rather the office of the air? And anyhow can smoke be 'flung'? It is not difficult, with *The March of Literature* open at page 699, to discern in these passages of Eliot's all the worst faults of Tennyson, unexcused (for how slim is Eliot's volume!) by Tennysonian over-production.

Which is all wrong of course, we know it's all wrong. But it serves to emphasize, when we've regained our bearings, how very *special* Eliot's method was, how much a knowing compendium of Victorian poetic mannerisms, to both yield and withhold satisfactions for tastes trained on Victorian poetry, and to represent—this was Eliot's immediate subject—souls trapped in 19th century conventions. That that age was a trap is an insight readily accessible to a generation brought up, as Eliot's was not, completely outside it; in *The French Lieutenant's Woman* Mr John Fowles has built a best-seller on just that perception. And to Mr Fowles' readers of the 1970s T. S. Eliot seems not to speak; he seems, though they do not state it that way, 'Victorian'.

Mr Eliot first visited Pound's triangular sitting-room on 22 September, 1914; eight days later Pound had a typescript of 'Prufrock' in his hands: 'the best poem I have yet had or seen from an American'. Until that day the one good 'modern poem of any length that Pound could point to was Ford's 'On Heaven', which in the June 1914 *Poetry* he had called 'the best poem yet written in the "twentieth-century fashion".'[2]

> ... And so she stood a moment by the door
> Of the long, red car. Royally she stepped down,
> Settling on one long foot and leaning back
> Amongst her russet furs. And she looked round ...
> Of course it must be strange to come from England

Straight into Heaven. You must take it in,
Slowly, for a long instant, with some fear . . .
Now that *affiche*, in orange, on the kiosque:
'*Six Spanish bulls will fight on Sunday next
At Arles, in the arena*' . . . Well, it's strange
Till you get used to our ways. And, on the *Maîrie*,
The untidy poster telling of the *concours
De vers de soie*, of silkworms. The cocoons
Pile, yellow, all across the little Places
Of ninety townships in the environs
Of Lyons, the city famous for her silks.
What if she's pale? It must be more than strange,
After these years, to come out here from England
To a strange place, to the stretched-out arms of me,
A man never fully known, only divined,
Loved, guessed-at, pledged to, in your Sussex mud,
Amongst the frost-bound farms by the yeasty sea.

A long quotation; but 'it is absolutely the devil', as Pound noted, 'to try to quote snippets from a man whose poems are gracious impressions, leisurely, low-toned': in other words, from a man who hangs nothing, nothing at all, on memorable phrases. 'On Heaven' has hardly a memorable line; everything in Eliot clings to the memory; everyone can quote

Revive for a moment a broken Coriolanus

though not everyone (not anyone?) can say what it means ('Impenetrability!' said Humpty Dumpty, 'That's what *I* say!'). *Coriolanus*: roll it on your tongue: it is the poetry of (Pound's phrase, paraphrasing Ford) 'the opalescent word'.

To render the proportion between England and Heaven, Ford offers, without ever localizing it in a quotable epigram, the proportion between England and Southern France. Setting this on the page, he supposed that he had to in some sense *evade* the English language.

Denn nach Köln am Rheine
Geht die Procession,

he quotes in the 1913 Preface to his then collected poems,[3] with the English gloss, 'For the procession is going to Cologne on the Rhine', and the remark that you 'could not use the word procession in an English poem. It would not be literary.' For 'We have a literary jargon in which we must write. We *must* write in it or every word will "swear".' So you not only cannot translate Heine into English, you cannot write in English as Heine wrote in German. 'In France, upon the whole, a poet—and even a quite literary poet—can write in a language that, roughly speaking, any hatter can use. In Germany, the poet writes exactly as he speaks. And these facts do so much towards influencing the poet's mind. If we cannot use the word "procession" we are apt to be precluded from thinking about processions', which are 'very much part of the gnat-dance that modern life is'. So, of course, are cars; and Ford did manage to use the word 'car', meaning a vehicle powered by an internal combustion engine, luxurious but subject to 'puncturing of the tyres' and 'trouble with the engine and gear'. That 'long, red car' (in 1913) sums up the lady, her stylish wilful independence, much as in a pre-Raphaelite poem a caparison'd palfrey would characterize its rider; and the trouble it cost Ford to devise an idiom into which he could slip the word 'car'—the diffuse, leisurely sentences, the intimacy with the reader, the colloquial ease, the many—too many —words: this was trouble undertaken to the end that he might, in the phraseology of the preface, register his own times in terms of his own time. He refused to call it trouble. Over prose he took trouble. As for verse, 'as far as I am concerned, it just comes. I hear in my head a vague rhythm . . . and the rest flows out.' No wonder he did not think highly of 'Prufrock', if he supposed that it just flowed out, and if he noted, as he must have, that the word 'etherised' is not accommodated by the language as 'On Heaven' accommodates 'car', but smirks with grotesque shock. That for him, was a fault.

For there were never two contemporaries less equipped to understand one another than Eliot and Ford, unless Eliot and William Carlos Williams. Pound, who understood them both, called it, about 1958, 'no secret' that he had learned more from Ford than from anyone else'.[4] He had gone to London, he thought it worth remarking fifty years later, because 'Yeats knew more about writing than any contemporary', and 'had made lyrics out of a single sentence, with no word out of natural order'. This fact seems not to have been perceived by subsequent inspectors of the early Yeats. It means that the form of the sentence, for him, was a ceremony. The twenty-four line sentence that comprises 'He

Remembers Forgotten Beauty' invests itself, in a hieratic manner learned via Symons from Mallarmé, with arrogances of diction: jewelled crowns, dew-cold lilies, swords upon iron knees; or a six-line sentence made 'out of a mouthful of air' will compel the children's children of today's great and proud to aver that their forefathers lied. Amid such rites of celebration and exorcism words are confined from straying out of natural order by obedience to the steely will, that will no more compromise with facile inversions than with 'the great and their pride'; nothing, in such a poetry, is really natural, any more than were the words of the Latin Mass, though the Mass is not in Cicero's Latin. Of the seven Yeats poems Pound anthologized in *Confucius to Cummings* (preface dated June 1958), five consist of but one sentence, the others of but two, each with the imperial stance and 'no word out of natural order'.

Pound never learned to do what Yeats did. Partly, a ceremonious syntax was alien to his paratactic temperament. Partly, he got entoiled in Pre-Raphaelite diction; one may hazard, by way of Rossetti's translations of Dante. In 1910 Ford printed the 'Canzon: Of Incense' in the April *English Review*. His good-natured remark of a year later, that 'Mr Pound as often as not is so unacquainted with English idioms as to be nearly unintelligible',[5] may have been prompted by such a stanza as this:

> The censer sways
>   And glowing coals some art have
> To free what frankincense before held fast
> Till all the summer of the eastern farms
> Doth dim the sense, and dream up through the light,
> As memory, by new-born love corrected—
> With savour such as only new love knoweth—
> Through swift dim ways the hidden pasts recalleth.

Ford printed that Canzon; but when in the very hot summer of 1911 Ezra Pound walking up from Italy brought him an entire volume called *Canzoni*, just off the press and two-thirds of it in that kind of language, Ford gave emphasis to his critique by rolling on the floor.

He felt the errors of contemporary style to the point of rolling (physically, and if you look at it as mere superficial snob, ridicuously) on the floor of his temporary quarters in Giessen when my third volume displayed me trapped, fly-papered, gummed and strapped down in a jejune provincial effort to learn, *mehercule*, the stilted language that then passed for 'good English' in the arthritic milieu that held control of the respected British critical circles.

And 'that roll', Pound went on, 'saved me at least two years, perhaps more. It sent me back to my own proper effort, namely, toward using the living tongue.'[6]

Ford was in Giessen on a fool's errand, trying to get a German divorce. He was spending his time in part writing a novel (*Ladies Whose Bright Eyes*) about the middle ages; its premise was that ages do not radically differ, save in smells and cuisine and minor customs. He was also writing the verse of *High Germany*, which includes a 'Canzone A La Sonata: to E. P.'—

> What do you find to boast of in our age,
> To boast of now, my friendly sonneteer,
> And not to blush for, later? By what line
> Do you entrain from Mainz to Regions saner?
> Count our achievements and uplift my heart;
> Blazon our fineness, Optimist, I toil
> Whilst you crow cocklike. But I cannot see
>
> What's left behind us for a heritage
> For our young children? What but nameless fear?
> What creeds have we to teach, legends to twine
> Saner than spun our dams? . . .

Like the *bouts rimés* with which Ford used to amuse himself, this was likely dashed off on the spot to enforce a point: the point that you can set yourself an intricate formal puzzle derived from the troubadours, and in the course of solving it maintain an idiom unmistakeably based on the idiom of speech. The poem contains, moreover, a sharp perception: that Pound's Canzoni were less homages to the past than statements about the present. To claim, as they do, that various sorts of visionary experience are accessible now, and inflect a love felt today, is to issue a boast about today's possibilities, a boast which, Ford says, falsifies today. 'Optimist', he says, ascribing such jejunity no doubt to American optimism; Pound's word twenty-eight years later was 'provincial'.

'Is there something about the mere framing of verse, the mere sound of it in the ear, that it must at once throw its practitioner or devotee into an artificial frame of mind?' This question of Ford's belongs to the same year as Pound's visit to Giessen, and very likely to the same summer, since it is followed within half a page by what seems a para-phrase of an injunction to Pound:

> This is not saying that one should not soak oneself with the Greek traditions: study every fragment of Sappho; delve ages long in the works of Bertran de Born; translate for years the minnelieder of Walther von der Vogelweide. . . . Let us do anything in the world that will widen our percep-tions. We are the heirs of all the ages. But, in the end, I feel fairly assured that the purpose of all these pleasant travails is the right appreciation of such facets of our own day as God will let us perceive.

Sappho and Bertrans were enthusiasms of Pound's; Ford had himself translated (if not 'for years') from Walther von der Vogelweide. His version of 'Tandaradei' (published in *From Inland*, 1907) was capturing the idiom of speech—

> Under the lindens on the heather,
> There was our double resting-place,
> Side by side and close together
> Garnered blossoms, crushed, and grass
> Nigh a shaw in such a vale:
> Tandaradei,
> Sweetly sang the nightingale.

—in a way Pound might have taken for example, and didn't, when he made a version from Bertrans (published in *Exultations*, 1909)—

> Sith no thing is but turneth into anguish
> And each to-day 'vails less than yestere'en. . . .

Which is not to say that Ford had prepared an idiom that could receive Bertrans' ceremonious *Planh*. But he had demonstrated the practi-cability of certain criteria which, as Pound came to see, even a cere-monious idiom could observe. By 1914 Pound had rendered another poem of Bertrans' into a diction that sustains the ceremony while avoiding the tushery of ''vails' and 'yestere'en':

> . . . Of Audiart at Malemort,
> Though she with a full heart
> Wish me ill,
> I'd have her form that's laced
> So cunningly,

> Without blemish, for her love
> Breaks not nor turns aside.
> I of Miels-de-ben demand
> Her straight fresh body,
> She is so supple and young,
> Her robes can but do her wrong. . . .

Ford's injunctions, Ford's example, lay behind such straightforward-ness.[7]

Diction: that was Ford's donation: words a person might say, not book-words, and sequences a person might speak. This is not Imagism, whose canons have nothing to say about diction. The Imagist canons speak of getting the Image directly onto the page, of eschewing un-necessary words, and of avoiding the metric of the metronome. Behind them lies a mystique of immediate perception, the immediacy of which enjoins economy. Economy, immediacy, these were not Ford's concerns.

He was a prose writer in all his intuitions. He thought in passages of speech, blocked out. The effects he cherished require time in which to take hold. His poems run on. He 'refused' (Pound said, 1958) 'the imagist rock-drill, intent on his own *donné*, his own. They say no angel can carry more than one message, and the most important critical act of the half-century was in the limpidity of natural speech, driven toward the just word, not slopping down, as he aimed specifi-cally not to slop into the more ordinary Wordsworthian word.'[8]

'It's an odd thing how one changes,' commences 'The Starling':[9]

> It's an odd thing how one changes . . .
> Walking along the upper ranges
> Of this land of plains,
> In this month of rains,
> On a drying road where the poplars march along,
> Suddenly,
> With a rush of wings flew down a company,
> A multitude, throng upon throng,
> Of starlings,
> Successive orchestras of wind-blown song,
> Flung, like the babble of surf,
> On to the roadside turf—

The just words are 'march' and 'orchestras' and 'babble'. But such words aren't, as in an Imagist poem, the turning-points of revelation. In an Imagist poem the exact word is a psychic feat, cutting like a shaft of light, transforming what is presented. In the most famous of all Imagist poems, 'In a Station of the Metro', the key word, 'petals', is not descriptive but pivotal:

> The apparition of these faces in the crowd;
> Petals on a wet, black bough.

(And the theme of Imagism, as Pound clearly saw when he wrote his second Canto, is metamorphosis: one thing, before the mind's eye, becoming another.)

Ford's starlings do not in this way effect a revelation. They remain starlings; and the poem goes on for another 85 lines to tell how one starling stayed behind to offer a virtuoso performance, but the poet didn't linger to enjoy it; and how in the village into which he wandered there was a wedding but he didn't stay to enjoy that either. Years ago, he says, he would have lingered for both. 'Yes, it's strange how one changes.'

These events are imagined like incidents in a novel. Juxtaposed, they do not state the poem's revelation; rather, they are occasions on which to meditate; meditating on them, the poet arrives at a revelation which he then explicitly states. It isn't a profound revelation, but the revelations at which one arrives by thinking seldom are. They need their specific occasions to lend them poignancy. And the function of exact unspectacular idiom, in 'The Starling', is to make the specific occasion real, and the poem's emotion therefore substantial.

To make the specific occasion real, and the poem's emotion therefore substantial, is Ford's normal poetic procedure. In a collection he published as early as 1904 he was evoking emotion by joining perception to perception—

> A bluff of cliff, purple against the south,
> And nigh one shoulder-top an orange pane.
> This wet, clean road; clear twilight held in the pools,
> And ragged thorns, ghost reeds and dim, dead willows.

> Past all the windings of these grey, forgotten valleys,
> To west, past clouds that close on one dim rift—
> The golden plains; the infinite, glimpsing distances,
> The eternal silences; dim lands of peace. . . .[10]

178 HUGH KENNER

Pound, for whom 'the natural object is *always* the adequate symbol', did not fail to notice an inconsistency in this poem's method: 'Don't use such an expression as "dim lands *of peace*",' he was advising neophytes in 1913. 'It dulls the image. It mixes an abstraction with the concrete.'[11] Though he didn't cite the poem nor name Ford, he was incidentally putting his finger on Ford's besetting poetic weakness. Having set down the specific occasion, he felt the need to interpret it, reflect on it, express its significance, and doing this would often betray his diction. 'Of peace' is a way of lending significance to 'dim lands', as the meditative narrative in 'The Starling' is a way to tell us what the song of the starling meant. 'Of peace,' however, is a shortcut, a verbal blur, whereas the reflective part of 'The Starling' is as cleanly written as the epiphanic part. When Ford succeeded he did so by clean writing; when he failed he did so by attempting a shortcut: as when, in 'Antwerp', he attempted to bring a solemn poem to the highest possible pitch in the final phrase, and instead smeared it with three terminal words: 'Oh poor dears!'

Once in his life he wrote a real Imagist poem.[12] It is frankly a day-dream from the trenches:

> Thank Goodness, the moving is over,
> They've swept up the straw in the passage
> And life will begin . . .
> This tiny, white, tiled cottage by the bridge!
> When we've had tea I will punt you
> To Paradise for the sugar and onions . . .
> We will drift home in the twilight,
> The trout will be rising.

'To Paradise for the sugar and onions'—that is the true Imagist metamorphosis. It is smoothly and cleanly done, and contrary to Ford's grain, for he seems never to have done anything like it again. His normal procedure is to develop, say, the life in the white cottage, and then in a separate passage to offer the explicit reflection that life there is what it must be to live in an outpost of Paradise. For he distrusted the speed of his imagination, and disciplined it to construct explicit set-pieces, or else indulged its flashes as casual whimsies.

A powerful tradition reinforced his distrust of imaginative leaps. Along with Kipling of the brassy finish and Hardy of the studied

awkwardness, he derives from Browning who derived from Words-
worth, who despite his friendship with Coleridge is not to be associated
with Coleridge, but with Crabbe and, standing behind Crabbe, the
Augustans; and behind them all stands Ben Jonson. This is the 'documentary' tradition, over against which, in the nineteenth century,
stood the 'aesthetic' tradition, Keats, Coleridge, Tennyson, Swinburne,
Yeats. It was the aesthetic tradition that absorbed Symbolism, so far as
English could absorb that highly French affair; out of that fusion stems
Eliot. The aesthetic tradition has so dominated critical thought that the
documentary tradition has gone unrecognized, and writers in the
documentary tradition have tended to be seen as inept aestheticians. I
know of no historian of these affairs, nor of anyone with a clear view of
the matter save Mr Basil Bunting, who has published no statement
about it. This paragraph has been based on his conversation.

Crabbe, then, somewhere behind Ford; and Ben Jonson behind them
both. When Ford writes of presenting his own time in terms of his own
time, of soaking oneself in learned traditions solely to the end of
appreciating rightly 'such facets of our own day as God will let us
perceive', he describes the procedure of the poet whose perception of
English life and language gave him a hyperbole for the number of
kisses bestowed—

> ... Till you equall with the store,
> All the grasse that Rumney yeelds,
> Or the sands in Chelsey fields,
> Or the drops in silver Thames,
> Or the starres, that guild his streams,
> In the silent sommer-nights,
> When youths ply their stolne delights

—which the learned will trace to Catullus vii,

> quam magnus numerus Libyssae harenae ...
> aut quam sidera multa, cum tacet nox,
> furtivos hominum vident amores

though Catullus offers only the format, not the instances. And so
thoroughly English is Jonson, so documentary, so enumerative, that
not till 1815 did anyone stumble on the fact that 'Drink to me only
with thine eyes' has a Greek original. *That* is Ford's notion of the way
to use learning; such is the power of tradition that though as far as I can

tell he gave Jonson's lyrics no thought, he may usefully be described as the last Jonsonian, with Jonson's notorious remarks about Donne as paradigm for his disesteem of Eliot.

Not that he took poetry seriously in Jonson's way; it was *writing* that he took seriously, and writing for him meant 'prose, that conscious and workable medium'. It is here that we may perceive the aesthetic tradition's damage: verse did not seem to Ford a conscious and workable medium. In the course of writing many thousand pages he sometimes wrote pages of verse, and was a little puzzled to know what to make of them. Only Pound knew: Pound who though likewise no esteemer of Jonson had much of Jonson's temperament, and who though the aesthetic tradition was in his blood had Browning likewise in his blood and so a predilection for the documentary. What Ford's didactic roll saved him from that day in Giessen was the decadence of aestheticism, and though to the end a high finisher of aesthetic detail, he set out to make his long poem out of facts, out of actualities, out of what his own time offered.

> I sat on the Dogana's steps
> For the gondolas cost too much, that year,
> And there were not 'those girls', there was one face,
> And the Buccentoro twenty yards off, howling 'Stretti',
> And the lit cross-beams, that year, in the Morosini,
> And peacocks in Koré's house, or there may have been.

—So Pound opening Canto III; and if 'those girls' is a homage to Browning, who had likewise sat on a Venetian step pondering Sordello, the idiom is not Browning's, it is Ford's, reminiscent. (And the reminiscence is Pound's.) The idiom of Canto I is archaic, 'The Seafarer'; the idiom of Canto II is metamorphic, the Imagist; the idiom of Canto III is colloquial, documentary, Ford's. These are the three principal threads in the warp of the *Cantos*, and it is the third that makes possible an extended poem that can utilize the other two.

NOTES

1. *The March of Literature* (1947) p. 699.

2. In an article reprinted as 'The Prose Tradition in Verse', *Literary Essays of Ezra Pound* (Norfolk, Conn., 1954) pp. 371–7.

3. The Preface is preserved as an appendix to the 1936 *Collected Poems*, pp. 323–42.

4. Ezra Pound and Marcella Spann, *Confucius to Cummings* (Norfolk, Conn., 1964) p. 327.

5. In the 1913 Preface; p. 342 of the 1936 edition.

6. 'Ford Madox (Hueffer) Ford; Obit.' in *Nineteenth Century and After*, CXXVI (Aug. 1939) pp. 178–81. [*Editor's note.*] See above p. 33.

7. The Bertrans versions, now both in *Personae*, are respectively 'Planh for the Young English King' and 'Dompna Pois de me No'os Cal.'

8. Pound and Spann, *Confucius to Cummings*, p. 327.

9. 'The Starling', in *High Germany* (1911).

10. 'On a Marsh Road (Winter Nightfall)', in *The Face of the Night* (1904).

11. 'Some Don'ts for Imagists', orginally composed as a rejection slip for *Poetry*. See *Literary Essays*, p. 5.

12. 'When the World was in Building', in *Poems Written on Active Service* (1918). Pound anthologized it in *Confucius to Cummings*, p. 304.

WILLIAM CARLOS WILLIAMS

To Ford Madox Ford in Heaven (1940)

Is it any better in Heaven, my friend Ford,
    than you found it in Provençe?

A heavenly man you seem to me now, never
    having been for me a saintly one.
It lived about you, a certain grossness that
    was not like the world.
The world is cleanly, polished and well
    made but heavenly man
is filthy with his flesh and corrupt that
    loves to eat and drink and whore—
to laugh at himself and not be afraid of
    himself knowing well he has
no possessions and opinions that are worth
    caring a broker's word about
and that all he is, but one thing, he feeds
    as one will feed a pet dog.

So roust and love and dredge the belly full
    in Heaven's name!
I laugh to think of you wheezing in Heaven.
    Where is Heaven? But why
do I ask that, since you showed the way?
    I don't care a damn for it
other than for that better part lives beside
    me here so long as I
live and remember you. Thank God you
    were not delicate, you let the world in
and lied! damn it you lied grossly

     sometimes. But it was all, I
  see now, a carelessness, the part of a man
   that is homeless here on earth.

  Provençe! the fat assed Ford will never
   again strain the chairs of your cafés,
  pull and pare for his dish your sacred garlic,
   grunt and sweat and lick
  his lips. Gross as the world he has left to
   us he has become
  a part of that of which you were the known
   part, Provençe, he loved so well.

SOURCE: W. C. Williams, *Collected Later Poems* (1944).

Select Bibliography

The best bibliographical aid is David Dow Harvey's annotated bibliography of the works and criticism (Princeton U.P., 1962). See also the current bibliography published periodically (since 1958) in *English Literature in Transition*, edited by Helmut E. Gerber. Richard M. Ludwig has edited Ford's letters (Princeton U.P., 1965), and Frank MacShane a selection of Ford's critical writings (Regents Critics Series, U. of Nebraska P., 1964).

Available biographies are Douglas Goldring, *The Last Pre-Raphaelite* (Macdonald, 1948; under title *Trained for Genius*: Dutton, 1949) and *South Lodge* (Constable, 1943); Frank MacShane, *The Life and Work of FMF* (Routledge & K. Paul, and Horizon Press, 1965); and Arthur Mizener, *The Saddest Story* (World Books, 1971). For personal accounts of Ford, see first Violet Hunt, *The Flurried Years* (Hurst & Blackett, 1926; under title *I Have This to Say*: Boni & Liveright, 1926), and Stella Bowen, *Drawn from Life* (Collins, 1941).

Several of Ford's books are again in print, but the only collection of his works is the four-volume Bodley Head edition (1962–63) edited and with valuable introductions by Graham Greene. Vol. I offers *The Good Soldier* and selections from Ford's reminiscences and poetry; Vol. II, the 'Fifth Queen' trilogy; Vols. III and IV, the Tietjens' novels, though *Last Post* is omitted.

Of the twelve critical books published on Ford in the past decade, nine are on the fiction alone. Richard A. Cassell, *FMF: A Study of His Novels* (Johns Hopkins, 1961), John Meixner, *FMF's Novels* (U. of Minnesota P., 1962), R. W. Lid, *FMF: The Essence of His Art* (U. of California P. at Berkeley, 1964), and Ambrose Gordon, Jr., *The Invisible Tent: The War Novels of FMF* (U. of Texas P., 1964) seek the technical, thematic and aesthetic patterns in Ford's fiction. Paul L. Wiley, *Novelist of Three Worlds: FMF* (Syracuse U.P., 1962), explores the cultural patterns as represented in Ford's fictional 'affairs'. Mrs Carol Ohmann, *FMF: From Apprentice to Craftsman* (Wesleyan U.P., 1964), studies the moral and psychological patterns in the fiction, and Robert J. Andreach, *The Slain and Resurrected God: Conrad, Ford and the Christian Myth* (New York U.P., 1970), the archetypal, religious patterns. Norman Leer, *The Limited Hero in the Novels of FMF* (Michigan State U.P., 1966), argues the changing nature of Ford's protagonists, and H. Robert Huntley, *The Alien Protagonist of FMF* (U. of North Carolina P., 1970), attempts to define the Fordian hero. Kenneth Young, *FMF* (Writers and Their Work, No. 74: Longmans, 1956), and Charles G. Hoffmann, *FMF* (English Authors Series: Twayne, 1968), contribute critical-biographical monographs dealing mostly with the fiction. Bernard J. Poli, *FMF and the Transatlantic Review* (Syracuse U.P., 1967), examines Ford's editorship of that journal.

A few useful and mostly recent items, other than those included in this volume, are:

W. Allen, *The English Novel* (Phoenix House, 1954; Dutton, 1955).

D. R. Barnes, 'Ford and the "Slaughtered Saints": A New Reading of *The Good Soldier*', in *Modern Fiction Studies*, XIV (1968).

T. K. Bender, 'The Sad Tale of Dowell: FMF's *The Good Soldier*', in *Criticism*, IV (1962).

R. P. Blackmur, 'The King Over the Water: Notes on the Novels of F. M. Hueffer', in *Princeton U. Library Chronicle*, IX (1948).

F. Bornhauser, 'Ford as an Art Critic', in *Shenandoah*, IV (1953).

B. D. Bort, '*The Good Soldier*: Comedy or Tragedy?', in *Twentieth Century Literature*, XII (1967).

M. Bronner, 'FMF: Impressionist', in *Bookman* (New York), XLIV (1916).

J. T. Cox, 'Ford's Passion for Provence', in *English Literary History*, XXVIII (1961).

A. Gordon Jr., '*Parade's End*: Where War was Fairy Tale', in *Texas Studies in Language and Literature*, V (1963).

Caroline Gordon, *A Good Soldier: A Key to the Novels of FMF* (Chapbook No. 1, U. of California Library at Davis, 1963).

E. B. Gose, Jr., 'Reality to Romance: A study of Ford's *Parade's End*', in *College English*, XVII (1956).

——'The Strange Irregular Rhythm: An Analysis of *The Good Soldier*', in PMLA, LXII (1957).

G. Greene, *The Lost Childhood* (Eyre, 1951; Viking, 1952).

—— Review of *Vive le Roy* in *London Mercury*, XXXVI (1937).

—— Review of *Provence* in *London Mercury*, XXXIX (1938).

J. Hafley, 'The Moral Structure of *The Good Soldier*', in *Modern Fiction Studies*, V (1959).

T. A. Hanzo, 'Downward to Darkness', in *Sewanee Review*, LXXIV (1966).

S. Hynes, 'Ford and The Spirit of Romance', *Modern Fiction Studies*, IX (1963).

A. Kennedy, 'Tietjens' Travels: *Parade's End* as Comedy', in *Twentieth Century Literature*, XVI (1970).

H. Kenner, *The Poetry of Ezra Pound* (New Directions, 1953).

—— *Gnomon* (McDonald, Oblensky, 1958).

R. M. Ludwig, *The Reputation of Ford Madox Ford*, PMLA, LXXVI (1961).

J. McCormick, *Catastrophe and Imagination: An Interpretation of the Recent English and American Novels* (Longmans, 1957).

T. Moser, 'Towards *The Good Soldier:* Discovery of a Sexual Theme', in *Daedulus*, LXXXXII (1963).

C. N. Pondrom, 'Hulme's "A Lecture on Modern Poetry" and the Birth of Imagism', in *Papers in Language and Literature*, V (1969).

E. Pound, *Polite Essays* (New Directions, 1937).

—— *Literary Essays*, ed. T. S. Eliot (New Directions, 1954).

V. S. Pritchett, Review of *Mightier Than the Sword* in *London Mercury*, XXXVIII (1938).

—— 'Fordie', in *New Statesman and Nation*, LXIII (22 June 1962).

—— 'Talented Agrarians', in *New Statesman and Nation*, LXVI (2 Aug 1963).

D. Scott, 'In Defence of Henry James', in *Bookman* (London), XLV (1914).

S. J. Stang, 'A Reading of Ford's *The Good Soldier*', in *Modern Language Quarterly*, XXX (1969).

L. Stevenson, *Yesterday and After* (Vol. XI of E. A. Baker's *The History of the English Novel*; Barnes & Noble, 1968).

M. D. Zabel, *Craft and Character in Modern Fiction* (Viking, 1957).

Notes on Contributors

Jo-Ann Baernstein, Lecturer in English and Drama, Brock University, Ontario, Canada; particularly interested in Ford Madox Ford's prophetic works.

Edward Crankshaw, Correspondent on Soviet affairs for *The Observer*, 1947–68; author of *Joseph Conrad: Some Aspects of His Art* (1936), the novels *Nina Lessing* (1938) and *What Glory* (1940), and *The Fall of the House of Habsburg* (1963) and *Maria Theresa* (1969).

Marlene Griffith, on the faculty of Laney College, Oakland, California; co-editor of *Borzoi College Reader* (2nd ed., 1971).

Samuel Hynes, Chairman, Department of English, Northwestern University; author of *The Pattern of Hardy's Poetry* (1961) and *The Edwardian Turn of Mind* (1968); editor of *Further Speculations* by T. E. Hulme (1955), *The Author's Craft and Other Writings* by Arnold Bennett (1968) and *Romance and Realism* by Christopher Caudwell (1970).

Hugh Kenner, Professor of English, University of California at Santa Barbara; publications include *The Poetry of Ezra Pound* (1953), *Wyndham Lewis* (1954), *Gnomon* (1958) and *Samuel Becket* (1968).

R. W. Lid, Chairman, Department of English, San Fernando Valley State College; author of *Ford Madox Ford: The Essence of His Art* (1964) and several textbooks.

John A. Meixner, Professor of English, Rice University, author of *Ford Madox Ford's Novels* (1962) and articles in *Kenyon, Southern, Sewanee Reviews,* and *College English.*

Ezra Pound, American poet and critic.

Mark Schorer, Professor of English, University of California at Berkeley; publications include *William Blake: The Politics of Vision* (1946) and *Sinclair Lewis: An American Life* (1961).

Melvin Seiden, Professor of English, State University of New York at Binghampton; author of short stories in *Epoch* and *The Southwest Review.*

William Carlos Williams (1883–1963), American poet, essayist, and fiction writer.

Morton Dauwen Zabel (1901–64), late Professor of English, the University of Chicago; publications include *Literary Opinion in America* (1937; revised 1951) and *Craft and Character in Modern Fiction* (1957).

Index